MASTERING THE
5 CORE VALUES

TO ACHIEVE GREATNESS

Gain Clarity, Experience Your Purpose, and Live Ideally

THE YEARN ADVANTAGE

Sherrie Rose

ISBN   978-0-9993747-4-0   *Print*
        978-0-9993747-5-7   *eBook*

This publication is designed to provide accurate and authoritative information about the subject matter covered. It is sold with the understanding that the publisher is not engaged in rendering legal, accounting, or other professional advice. If legal advice or other expert assistance is required, the services of a competent professional should be sought. The opinions expressed by the author in this book are the sole responsibility of the author rendering the opinion.

First Printing Edition, May 2023

Subjects: Self-Management | Creative ability in business | Personal Growth |

Available from Author's website, Amazon.com, and other retail outlets.

Available at special quantity discounts for bulk purchases for sales promotions, premiums, fundraising, and educational use. Special versions or book excerpts can also be created to fit specific needs.

For more information, please contact:
https://belegacyworthy.com

Dedication

**To All Who Dream
of
Achieving Greatness**

*Your Puzzle Piece
May be Your Masterpiece*

Table of Contents

MASTERING THE
5 CORE VALUES
TO ACHIEVE GREATNESS

THE YEARN ADVANTAGE

Foreword

AS a seasoned expert in the crowded personal development and business coaching and consulting space, I have had the privilege of working with many individuals and teams dedicated to growing and achieving their goals. One of the most important lessons I have learned over the years is the importance of establishing core values in achieving success.

I am thrilled to introduce *Mastering the 5 Core Values: The YEARN Advantage*, a book that will help you discover and develop the essential values necessary for achieving your goals and reaching your full potential.

'Mastering the 5 Core Values' is divided into several parts, with one part required reading and the others as supporting chapters. This approach allows you to tailor your reading experience to your needs and interests and get to the core in 5 minutes. Seriously, in 5 minutes!

Part I of the book, 'The Key Questions to Ask,' will get your mental gears turning and provide you with nuggets of wisdom to ponder. Part II, the required reading section, 'Discover the 5 Core Values', will help you understand the book's main ideas and concepts. Parts III, IV, and V, the supporting chapters, provide a deeper dive into specific topics related to the main ideas of the YEARN Advantage.

Sherrie Rose's unique approach to goal setting in Part V, 'Purpose & Mission are Led by Vision', provides an exciting perspective to envision grand ideas when you are open and ready to dream BIG. It expands your understanding of the concept and helps you to think critically about additional insights and perspectives into creating on a grand scale.

This book is a valuable resource when you are looking to grow personally and professionally. Following along in the book, *Mastering the 5 Core Values'*, you can fully engage with the YEARN Advantage and develop the essential values that lead you to greatness.

I highly recommend this book to anyone who is serious about achieving their goals, reaching their potential, and living fully.

Let the discovery begin!

Heart-to-Heart,

Dr. Terri Levine

Chief Heart-repreneur®
Best-selling author of over 40 books
Business mentoring expert with heart
www.Heartrepreneur.com

Preface

During the Covid pandemic, I had the pleasure of partnering with Coen Tan from Singapore. During our weekly Zoom meetings, we collaborated and supported each other. We created various models and frameworks and brainstormed.

Often during these meetings, we would be reviewing slides. Find one of these slides shown in Part III of the book, titled 'YEARN in Review.' Yes, you read that right.

After looking at the slide, Coen remarked, "Way to bury the lead! That's brilliant! That needs to be on its own. Write a book on it." Then he quoted Clare Luce, "The height of sophistication is simplicity."

My simple YEARN slide is the genesis of this book: Mastering the 5 Core Values. Read along to achieve greatness, gain clarity, experience your purpose, and live ideally.

The simplicity of my concept concerned me, but Coen assuaged my fears. People may perceive a concept as unimportant if anyone can understand it. There can be a tendency to equate complexity with importance and simplicity with triviality.

This brings up a saying attributed to Albert Einstein, "Make everything as simple as possible, but not simpler." Oversimplification can obscure important details or nuances.

Einstein, known for the theory of relativity, cites this as a guiding principle for scientific and creative endeavors. It emphasizes the importance of simplicity and clarity in communication and problem-solving.

The YEARN Advantage is straightforward and memorable. It's easy to explain and will capture your attention. The simplicity of the concept encourages greater engagement and resonance.

Steve Jobs, a co-founder of Apple Inc., was well known for his sleek and simple design sensibility. Jobs' design sensibility was a critical factor in Apple's success.

Jobs said, "Simple can be harder than complex: You have to work hard to get your thinking clean to make it simple. But it's worth it in the end because once you get there, you can move mountains."

To communicate complex ideas is a hallmark of mastery and expertise. Simplification is distilling complex ideas into clear and concise language. This requires deep comprehension of the subject matter. Simplification helps make information more accessible and relevant to a broader audience.

I would love you to apply the insights of the YEARN Advantage presented and repeated in different forms throughout this book. You will be on your way to mastering your greatness.

How To Read This Book

BY following this guide on how to read the book in your hands, 'Mastering the 5 Core Values,' you will fully engage with the YEARN Advantage. It is my hope that this book will be your valuable personal and professional resource.

The Introduction: *Recommended*

This introduction contains essential information for understanding this book's main ideas and concepts. It ties in personal agency and *'Mastering the 5 Core Values'*.

Part I - *Recommended:* The Key Questions to Ask

The Key Questions cover personal, business, and the big meta questions. These are fun and thought-provoking questions. The idea in this chapter is to get your mental gears turning. You'll find nuggets of wisdom in these questions.

Part II - *REQUIRED:* Discover the 5 Core Values

This section asks questions that relate to the YEARN Advantage and are the keys to *'Mastering the 5 Core Values'*. Here you will discover and gain an understanding of the main ideas and concepts of this book. Read this section thoroughly before moving on to the supporting chapters. You'll find the five values repeated in different formats and contexts to help reinforce learning and retention.

Part III- *Recommended:* Mastery and The YEARN Advantage

You'll read practical examples and stories related to the main ideas discussed in the required section. This section will help you apply the concepts covered in the book to real-life scenarios. There is also a one-page at-a-glance snapshot that is beneficial. There is a set of questions to be used as a reference for each of the five core values.

Part IV - *Supporting Chapter:* Delving Deeper into YEARN

Take a deeper dive into specific topics related to the main ideas of the YEARN Advantage. You'll get a more comprehensive understanding of the concepts covered in the book to help expand your thinking, as they say, "out of the box."

Part V- *Supporting Chapter:* Purpose & Mission are Led by Vision

This section provides a unique approach to goals, objectives, and big dreams. It introduces *enhavim* using several models to help visualize the concept for planning at scale. If you are a big dreamer, this section will help you hone your critical thinking skills, broaden your understanding, and give you new insights and perspectives.

Final Touches - *Supporting Chapters*

Discover further resources and references related to the book's main ideas. This will help you expand your knowledge and continue learning beyond this book.

Introduction

WHY would you choose to read a new book on personal mastery and self-development when many books are readily available on this topic?

Unique perspective: Even if the topic is the same, every author has their way of presenting the information. My approach gives you, my dear reader, a fresh perspective and new insights. Concepts are easy to grasp and follow Einstein's criterion, *"When you can explain it to a 6-year-old, it's a sign that you truly understand it."*

Specific focus: Personal development books provide a different focus which cater to the reader's interests. Some may concentrate on emotional intelligence, for example, while others focus on building better habits or managing stress. *Mastering the 5 Core Values* is a simplified framework. As Golding said, *"The greatest ideas are the simplest."*

Personal recommendation: People often turn to books because someone they trust recommended them. Hearing from a friend or colleague who has already read and benefited from my book can be a compelling reason to read it. In turn, you'll tell a friend.

On my behalf, please thank the person who recommended *Mastering the 5 Core Values* to you.

Mastering the 5 Core Values and Personal Agency

The information presented in this book can help you develop your personal agency. You can take charge of your life, strive for your goals, and create the life you yearn for.

Personal Agency and *Mastering the 5 Core Values* are complementary concepts. Each emphasize the importance of taking ownership of one's life, making intentional choices, and pursuing a fulfilling lifestyle.

Mastering the 5 Core Values provides a framework for individuals. You can learn how to develop a solid sense of self, take consistent action toward goals, leverage resources, build a network of like-minded individuals, and create an environment that supports growth.

Human agency is about having the power to make choices and exert our will in society at large. In contrast, personal agency is about an individual's ability to make choices and take action in their own life. Personal agency is necessary for personal freedom, autonomy, and well-being. It allows individuals to pursue aspirations, build meaningful relationships, and achieve dreams.

To master personal agency and achieve greatness, align your goals with your values, obtain necessary resources, and build meaningful connections by collaborating with others. This will aid you in pursuing personal greatness.

Personal **Agency** is the power to make choices and take actions that shape our lives and circumstances.

To act intentionally and purposely involves making decisions based on our values and convictions and taking responsibility for the outcomes. There may be external pressures or constraints that could limit your ability to act on your behalf.

Personal agency is about crafting your destiny. Personal agency is the ability to take charge of your life and make choices that take charge of your future. It involves managing your thoughts, feelings, and behaviors, so you can make decisions based on your beliefs and values. When you exercise personal agency, you direct your life by aligning your choices with your actions and strategic plans.

The power to act on your own accord is essential for living a life full of meaning. Making decisions based on your values and convictions, and accepting responsibility for the consequences, gives you a sense of control over your destiny. Exercising independence and making choices consistent with your values can boost your empowerment.

Personal agency enables individuals to pursue their aspirations, build meaningful relationships, and accomplish important goals.

Personal agency is a significant factor in establishing a life with purpose and happiness.

Personal agency is vital in various aspects of life, including education, the workplace, health and more. In education, personal agency allows you to take charge of your learning, set goals, and take responsibility for your progress. In the workplace, personal agency can help you gain autonomy and control over your work, leading to higher job satisfaction and productivity. In health, personal agency enables individuals to take responsibility for their well-being, make healthy choices, and manage their healthcare.

Personal agency also requires a stimulating environment that encourages individuals to exercise their freedom and skills.

Mastering the 5 Core Values to achieve greatness helps you develop beyond personal agency to gain clarity, experience your purpose, and live ideally. These five core values are the YEARN Advantage.

The YEARN Advantage is the key to mastering your personal agency and achieving greatness. By following the YEARN five core values, you can unlock your ambitions and build the life of your dreams. This can include setting up an environment that promotes and motivates, using resources effectively, investing in yourself and your future, and collaborating with others to bring creativity and innovation.

PART
I

The Key Questions to Ask

K EY questions are essential as you strive for personal growth and a deeper understanding of yourself and the world around us. People who engage in self-inquiry are motivated to grow and evolve and are willing to act toward their self-awareness.

Below are some reasons why it is important to ask key questions about life:

To gain clarity: Asking key questions can help us clarify our values, beliefs, and goals. When we ask honest questions about what matters to us, what we want to achieve, and what makes us happy, we can better understand our priorities and make decisions that align with them.

To increase self-awareness: Self-awareness is essential for your development. By asking key questions about our strengths, weaknesses, and behavior patterns, we can gain a deeper understanding of ourselves and our motivations.

To challenge assumptions: Asking key questions can help us challenge our assumptions and biases. By questioning our beliefs and perspectives, we can gain a broader and more nuanced understanding of the world and the people around us.

To foster creativity and innovation: Asking key questions can stimulate creativity and innovation by encouraging us to think outside the box and explore new possibilities. We can generate new ideas and approaches by questioning the status quo and imagining new solutions.

To find meaning and purpose: Asking key questions can help us find meaning and purpose in our lives. Reflecting on our values and goals, we can identify what matters most and work towards a fulfilling and meaningful life.

Regularly review the key questions about life and business as an essential practice for personal growth and business development. These questions can lead to a more prosperous life and successful business.

In Part II, "Discover the 5 Core Values," you'll read the chapter about people. There is a section on how to ask and answer better questions for better communication.

Next are the Personal Key Questions, then the Business Questions, followed by the big Meta Questions.

You'll find these questions in various forms repeated throughout the book.

Personal Questions

7 KEY QUESTIONS are straightforward; each question relates to the five core values. After you read on and discover the five core values, return here and match each question to the value.

Bonus if you send your answer to us: yearn @ BeLegacyWorthy.com

Questions for YOU

1. Who are you? What is your Identity?
2. What do you want to do?
3. Why do you want to do it?
4. What do you need to do it?
5. Where do you want to be?
6. What conversation(s) do you want to be in?
7. Who do you want to associate with?

These personal questions fall into three general categories:

A. 'Personal Transformation'

Your Development and Growth. You have the courage and commitment to change for the better. Your beliefs resonate deeply and aid in fine-tuning the direction of your compass. Congratulate yourself on reading this book. It shows your curiosity and yearning for self-improvement. YAY, you!

B. 'Your Place in the World'

Your Self-Worth. These are the base values of who you are. This is what you do, the tools and resources you can access, where you belong, and what satisfies you personally. Your daily actions and where you live in the world.

C. 'Community Outreach'

Beyond You. Life is about people and your relationships. Being of service and committed to others. The meaning in your life derives from the common good and future generations. You quickly follow your moral compass to guide you forward.

Business Questions

Key Questions for BUSINESS

The genesis of these questions comes from Rob Nixon and his company, 'PROFITABLE PARTNERS'

These five questions from Rob Nixon of Australia were crafted when he was ousted from the company he built. The board of directors wanted him out, and he started over with a new company. *Rob's preliminary question was:*

If you had a blank sheet of paper to design the business of your dreams - what would it look like?

1. What do you want YOUR business life to look like?

2. What annual revenue would you like to generate?

3. What type of work do you want to do (products or services)?

4. What type of culture do you want to create?

5. Whom do we deliver the above services?

Note: The questions above are modified from Rob Nixon's original set. Each business question relates to one of the five core values. If you are an entrepreneur or are starting a business, after you read on and discover the five core values, return here and match the question to the value. **Bonus** if you send your answers to us at: yearn @ BeLegacyWorthy.com

Meta Questions

META QUESTIONS - The big, metaphysical, mind-bending philosophical questions about the nature of existence, reality, and our place in the universe. Meta is when the subject itself is the object of reflection.

The meta questions do not specifically relate to the five core values but are intriguing! This book is about creating a better "you." These meta questions are good "food for thought" in the creative process.

Have you ever wondered about these Meta questions?

1.   What is the meaning of life?

The meaning of life is a philosophical question that seeks to understand the purpose or significance of human existence. It can vary depending on individual beliefs, values, and experiences.

This is one of the fundamental questions that humans ask across most cultures. It touches on issues of purpose, significance, and value. This question has been pondered by thinkers and philosophers throughout history.

2.   What is the origin of the universe?

The universe's origin is a scientific and philosophical question that seeks to explain how the universe began. The Big Bang Theory is a widely accepted scientific theory that explains the origin of the universe.

3. What is the nature of reality?

The nature of reality is the study of what exists and how it can be known. This includes examining the nature of physical matter, the universe, consciousness, and perception.

4. What is the nature of consciousness?

The nature of consciousness is a philosophical question that asks what it means to be aware and experience the world around us. It involves studying the relationship between the brain and the mind and how consciousness emerges from physical processes.

5. What is the nature of free will?

The nature of free will is a philosophical question that asks whether humans can make choices not predetermined by external factors. It is related to the concepts of determinism, causation, and personal responsibility.

6. Is there a purpose to our existence?

The purpose of our existence is an intensely debated philosophical and religious question. Some believe our existence has a specific purpose or destiny, while others think we create our purpose. You decide.

7. What is the relationship between the mind and the body?

The relationship between the mind and the body is philosophical and scientific. It asks how mental processes are related to physical processes. It involves studying the brain, consciousness, and the physical world.

8. What is the role of human beings in the universe?

The role of human beings in the universe is a philosophical and scientific question that examines the place of humans in the natural world. It considers our environmental impact, relationships with other species, and the search for greater meaning and purpose.

9. What is the nature of good and evil?

The nature of good and evil is a philosophical and ethical question. It examines the concepts of right and wrong, morality, and the nature of human behavior. Cultural, religious, and societal norms influence these concepts.

10. What is reality?

This question asks whether the world we experience is an objective reality or a construct of our minds. It has implications for our understanding of the nature of consciousness, perception, and truth.

11. Is there a God or a higher power?

This question asks whether there is a higher power or supernatural force that governs the universe. It has implications for morality, ethics, religion, and the purpose of existence.

12. What is the nature of consciousness?

This question asks how our subjective experiences arise from the brain's physical processes. It has implications for understanding free will, self-awareness, and the mind-body problem.

13. What is the nature of time?

This question asks whether time is an objective feature of the universe or a human construct. It has implications for our understanding of causality, determinism, and the nature of the universe. We will discuss the concept of time later in the book as it relates to one of the five core values.

There are many other philosophical questions, and the answers are often complex and contested. Some of these meta questions may not have definitive answers. These meta questions are difficult to answer. Philosophers, scientists, theologians, and other thinkers have grappled with them for centuries. The pursuit of answers to these questions is what drives human curiosity and exploration.

PART II

Discover the 5 Core Values

YEARN. To yearn is a deep feeling that can go beyond a simple desire or need. To yearn may encompass a profound longing for connection, purpose, or fulfillment in life.

YEARN is an acronym or word mnemonic for memory retention for the five core values. The image of the YEARN apple core slices represent the five core values to achieve greatness.

A yearning and a desire are similar but with some subtle differences.

A desire is a general feeling of wanting or wishing for something, often driven by a need or a want. A desire can be a conscious or unconscious urge. A desire is for something, such as material possessions, experiences, or emotions. Personal goals, societal norms, or cultural expectations all motivate desire.

In contrast, 'to yearn' refers to a strong and sincere longing for something. It can involve a sense of incompleteness in one's current state. Yearn can be a powerful craving to attain or experience something meaningful.

A yearning may focus on a future possibility. A solid emotional longing may seem barely out of reach yet remain coveted. Yearning for your dreamed outcome is a powerful pull, even if there are obstacles in the way. This type of yearning can be frustrating as you work toward the desired future you want to achieve.

A person may yearn to have a successful career in a competitive field but feel they lack the means or opportunities to make it happen. They may have a deep longing for the future they imagine, with all its potential rewards and possibilities, yet struggle to find a way to make it a reality. This type of yearning has challenges and can be both encouraging and discouraging. The yearning inspires ambition but causes dissatisfaction or disillusionment with the current situation.

Yearning about having a dream of a better life is a powerful emotional longing for a life that is different from one's current reality. It is a feeling of intense desire and a deep sense of purpose, often driven by the belief that life can be improved or transformed in a meaningful way. Personal growth, financial stability, or greater happiness and fulfillment can motivate the yearning.

Yearning for happiness is not a fixed destination or endpoint but a journey or direction you can pursue throughout your life. Happiness cannot be achieved 'once and for all' but rather a continuous process of growth and self-discovery.

Happiness is not dependent on external circumstances or material possessions. It cannot be bought, sold, or acquired with resources through external means. Instead, happiness is a state of mind, a way of being in the world rooted in your inner sense of well-being and contentment.

By framing happiness as a direction rather than a place, it is an ongoing process of self-discovery. You can work towards it but only sometimes arrive at it. You may experience moments of happiness along the way, but the yearning for happiness is an ongoing journey.

This idea can be liberating, as it takes the pressure off that some yearnings like happiness do not have an endpoint. This can empower you to focus on your inner well-being and personal growth and find joy in pursuing your goals and aspirations.

A person may yearn for a better life, including financial security, a fulfilling career, and a sense of purpose. Yearning is fueled by a belief that the current circumstances do not reflect their true potential. It may be a deep-seated dissatisfaction with their current situation. Yearning may drive them to take action toward their goals. It may be yearning for further education, new job opportunities, or significant lifestyle changes.

Yearning and desire show up in different languages with various expressions. Hebrew and Greek have over fifty words for desire.

Yearning about having a dream of a better life is a solid emotional desire for longing for a more fulfilling, meaningful, and satisfying life. If the desired future may feel unattainable or elusive, it may be accompanied by frustration or despair. There may be a deep dissatisfaction or discontent with one's current circumstances, and this wanting can spurn a better future.

Yearning is often accompanied by a vision of a different and improved reality. This may involve changes in relationships, career, lifestyle, or personal growth. There may be a feeling of a deep sense of longing for a life that is more aligned with your values, passions, and aspirations. This type of yearning can be motivating, as it requires significant dedication to turn the dream into a reality.

Yearning for a better life represents the possibility for growth, change, and transformation. To yearn can create a sense of hopefulness and optimism.

Y.E.A.R.N. is an acronym that stands for the five core values that can help you live to your fullest potential. It's about having a solid sense of self and standing up for what is essential to YOU. ENVIRONMENT combines your physical, digital, and social aspects and how they shape your experience. ACT refers to action toward your goals through sustained effort and a positive mindset. RESOURCES are the tangible and intangible tools you have access to help you reach your goals. NETWORKS is about connecting with people who share your passions, interests, and ambitions. #tyadvantage

Skip to 'YEARN in Review' for a snapshot view on one page.

5 CORE VALUES: Understanding the five core values lets you clarify what matters most and make decisions leading to a more fulfilling life. The five core values enable you to live in the way and place of your choosing and experience a deeper purpose. This helps your life travel in the right direction, and you feel a sense of success. Apply the five core values to progress toward the attainment of your goals while forming meaningful connections. With these five core values, you have the power to create a life full of satisfaction and joy!

Y.E.A.R.N.

1. **(Y) YOU** - The first core value of the YEARN Advantage is YOU. This represents your personal physical, emotional, mental, and spiritual motivators. Understanding what drives you and motivates you to achieve your goals is essential. By asking, for example, "Why do I want to achieve this goal?" you can determine your purpose and motivation. This question helps you to explore your inner drive and passion for your goals, which can help you stay committed and focused.

2. **(E) ENVIRONMENT** - The second core value of the YEARN Advantage is Environment. This refers to the places you occupy in the natural world, offline, and the digital world, online. This core value is critical because it can affect productivity, creativity, and well-being. By asking, "Where will this goal be achieved?" you can take steps to improve your surroundings. Identify potential distractions that may hinder you. Find situations that enhance activity. This question helps you assess your environment and make necessary changes to support your goals.

3. **(A) ACTIONS** - The third core value of the YEARN Advantage is Actions. This represents the steps you take to achieve your goals. Defining your actions with criteria, realism, and a plan and timeline is essential to increase your chances of success. By asking, "What do I want to accomplish?" and "When do I want to achieve this goal?" you can establish a clear plan to act upon. These questions also help you determine your goals' feasibility and set a deadline for achievement.

4. **(R) RESOURCES** - The fourth core value of the YEARN Advantage is Resources. This represents the monetary and intangible requirements to make progress on your actions. You must understand the resources you need to achieve your goals and determine if they are available. By asking, "What do I need to achieve this goal?" and "Do I have the resources and capabilities to achieve the goal? If not, what am I missing?" you can identify what resources you require and plan accordingly. This question helps you to determine if you need to acquire new skills, seek financial support, or leverage existing resources.

5. **(N) NETWORKS** - The fifth core value of the YEARN Advantage is Networks. This represents the individuals and communities who will support and facilitate your actions. Building a support network can help you stay accountable, and motivated. People in your networks may connect you to valuable resources. You can identify potential collaborators and supporters by asking, "Who now is involved in this goal?" "Who can we engage with in the future?" These questions can help you connect with like-minded individuals and receive helpful feedback and support.

By activating The YEARN Advantage, you can clarify, organize, and focus your efforts toward achieving your goals.

Find your purpose to achieve greatness. Unlock your ambitions. Nurture your environment. Take action. Maximize your resources. Form beneficial collaborations. Establish a clear action plan by answering the questions corresponding to the five core values.

The YEARN Advantage is here to help you. It will help you clarify, organize and focus your efforts. The five core values is a framework structured to help you develop personally and professionally. It emphasizes knowing yourself, making plans, and taking action. It emphasizes self-awareness, planning, and execution. Answer the five questions corresponding to each core value and establish a clear action plan. Evaluate your progress, adjust accordingly, and find your purpose to achieve greatness.

The hashtag *#tyadvantage* represents The YEARN Advantage. In it are the letters TY which for many represent the words "Thank You." Thank yourself for investing in yourself. Having gratitude is an admirable quality and is recommended as a daily practice.

In this book, some concepts may be repeated in different ways. If you think, "I've read this before," it's a good sign that you understand the information, and it is sinking in.

"Repetition makes us familiar with what we know.
It is a necessary condition for the formation of
habits, whether intellectual or moral."
~William James

Y - Whose Life is it anyway?

"The best investment you can make is in yourself."
~ Warren Buffet

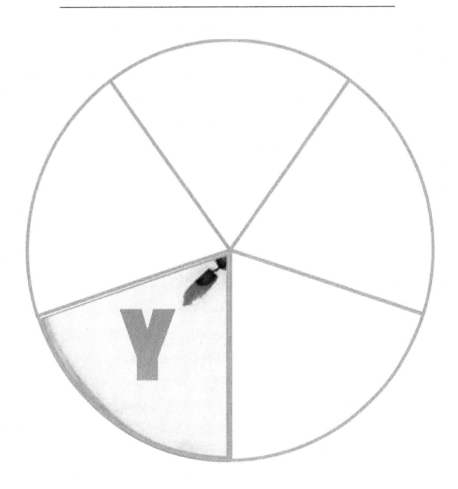

YOU (SELF)
IS CORE VALUE #1

"You can unlock your ambitions and strive for greatness - Harness Your Power!"

You have the potential to reach greatness, and it begins by taking control of your life. The letter 'Y' in the YEARN advantage system stands for YOU, the individual. Step up and strive to reach your objectives, be innovative, accomplish your dreams, and ascend to new heights.

The 'Y' in YEARN symbolizes you and your potential. Let it remind you of who you are and your power. Challenge yourself to do amazing things, develop creative solutions, and realize your aspirations. Reach levels of success you never imagined.

"Life is not about finding yourself. Life is about creating yourself."

Lolly Daskal is the author of the quote above, often attributed to Nobel Prize winner George Bernard Shaw. Her quote suggests that the purpose of life is not to discover who you are but to actively shape and create your identity. It implies that we have the power to mold ourselves into the people we want to be and that our past or present circumstances do not limit us.

Many believe their identity is fixed and determined by genetics, upbringing, or life experiences. You can challenge that notion, redirect your life, and actively work towards becoming the best version of yourself.

Creating yourself involves a process of self-inquiry, self-discovery, self-reflection, and self-improvement. It means identifying your strengths and weaknesses, setting goals, and taking action to achieve them. It also means embracing change and being willing to learn from your mistakes; mistakes can be your best teachers!

We are not passive observers of our lives but active participants. Self-creation is an intentional and dynamic process. Instead of waiting for our identity to be handed to us, we have the power and responsibility to shape it ourselves.

We can choose our thoughts, beliefs, and actions and therefore affect our destinies. Life is not a journey of self-discovery but a journey of self-creation.

The idea of "finding oneself" can imply that we are born with a predetermined destiny or purpose. Our identities are not fixed but constantly evolving based on our experiences and choices. We can create the person we want to be.

I suggest that the person you want to be is "legacy worthy." To "be legacy worthy" shows up in your actions which are today's reputation and, eventually, how you will be remembered.

Achieving greatness is not solely dependent on natural ability or intelligence. It factors in curiosity, energy, and a willingness to push yourself to the limit. By recognizing your potential and striving to make the most of it, you can achieve great things and positively impact the world.

Your relationship with yourself is essential to developing healthy, satisfying relationships with others. Taking care of ourselves is the key to creating meaningful relationships with others. Recognize the link between yourself and others to help address underlying issues or insecurities. It helps build greater self-acceptance and comfort. When you nurture your relationship with yourself, you can create a strong foundation for forming positive connections with others. This leads to more fulfilling relationships and greater well-being.

Creating yourself requires introspection and self-awareness. Take time to understand your strengths, weaknesses, values, and beliefs. You can intentionally mold your identity. It also involves taking risks, trying new things, and learning from our mistakes. By actively creating yourself, you can become the best version of yourself and live a more fulfilling life.

YOU, Character Traits, and Virtues

Character traits and virtues are crucial aspects of an individual's personality and behavior. There are differences between traits and virtues, and some overlap. Character traits can be positive or negative, while virtues are always positive.

Character traits are inherent qualities or tendencies that an individual possesses. Character traits describe a person's natural tendencies. They influence how an individual behaves in different situations.

Virtues are desirable moral or ethical qualities that are considered to be universally good. They are often seen as ideals to strive for and can help guide a person's behavior and decision-making. Virtues are more prescriptive of qualities to aspire to. Virtues can help individuals become better versions of themselves.

Positive character traits include honesty, kindness, empathy, and patience. Negative traits may consist of selfishness, dishonesty, and impulsivity. There are commonalities between character traits and virtues. Virtues include honesty, courage, justice, compassion, and wisdom. Many positive character traits, such as honesty and compassion, are also considered virtues.

Developing character traits and virtues is important. Practicing virtues can help individuals cultivate positive character traits. Positive character traits can help individuals live up to the *ideals* of the virtues.

THE ASPECTS OF LOVEMATISM:

The YOU value has four aspects, and most personal activity falls into one or a combination:

Physical Aspect: Taking care of your body and health by exercising, eating well, resting, and managing stress. —Your *body connection.*

Mental Aspect: Your mind helps you learn, create, solve problems, plan and make decisions. —Your *mind connection.*

Emotional Aspect: Your emotions, attitudes, and reactions are part of who you are. Being aware of yourself, your emotions, your drives. Being empathetic, and using social skills to build relationships. —Your *heart connection.*

Spiritual Aspect: Your existential soul of humanity. Having a sense of purpose, values, beliefs, ethics, and feeling connected to something larger than yourself. —Your *soul connection.*

You will see how almost everything in your personal life falls into one or more of these four aspects. This applies to how you relate to yourself and how you connect in a partnership.

The word lovematism was initially coined to describe the intense bond between lovers, where the body, heart, mind, and soul are connected. These aspects show up in shared experiences like daily routines, surprises, and new adventures. You can also experience these feelings when you activate the four aspects of lovematism within yourself.

First Questions for 'YOU'

- ## Who are you?
- ## What is your Identity?

To answer the questions "Who are you?" and **"What is your identity?"** it is worth noting that identity is a fluid and dynamic concept and may shift over time as a person's circumstances and experiences change. Many topics can be explored to understand your identity and how various external factors have affected you.

Personal History: Your personal history, including your upbringing, experiences, and relationships, affects your identity. Understanding your personal history can provide insight into how you see yourself and your place in the world. *Your mind and emotional connection.*

Values and Beliefs: Your values and beliefs are often integral to your identity. This can include your religious, political, and cultural beliefs and personal virtues, such as honesty, integrity, and compassion. *Your mind and emotional connection.*

Personality Traits: A person's identity can be defined by personality traits such as introversion, extroversion, emotional stability, and openness. *Your mind and emotional connection.*

Health: Your physical and mental health can significantly impact your identity. Awareness of your health status, including any chronic conditions or disabilities, may provide insight into how best to navigate and interact with others. *Your body and mental connection.*

Goals and Aspirations: Your goals and aspirations can also define your identity. Understanding what motivates and drives you can provide insight into who you are. *Your mental and spiritual connection.*

Resources-Money: The resources and money a person has access to can also shape your identity. This can include socioeconomic status, education, and career opportunities. This will be reviewed in the R core value.

Interests and Hobbies: Your interests and hobbies can also contribute to your identity. For example, someone passionate about music may see themselves as a musician or music lover. *Your mind and emotional connection.*

Family History: Your family history, including ancestry and cultural heritage. This can provide insight into how you see yourself and your place in the world. *Your mind and emotional connection.*

Country-Locale: The country or locale that a person is from can also be a defining aspect of their identity. This can include cultural norms, language, social structures, and political affiliations. This is reviewed in the E core value.

Race and Ethnicity: A person's race and ethnicity are part of their identity. Cultural background, experiences, and perspectives impact identity. *Your mind and emotional connection.*

Gender and Sexuality: Gender and sexuality are essential aspects of identity. This influences how a person sees themselves and how others perceive them. *Your body and emotional connection.*

Religion and Spirituality: Religion and spirituality can be integral to a person's identity. This influences belief systems and behaviors. *Your spiritual connection.*

Culture and Community: Culture and community can also play a significant role in molding one's identity. This relates to the environment you grew up in and where you live now. *Your emotional connection.*

Relationships: Your longest relationship is with yourself. A person's relationships with others, such as family, friends, and romantic partners, can also shape their identity. Understanding how relationships have influenced your self-perception can provide insight into identity. *Your emotional connection.*

Lovematism in Action

The four aspects of lovematism – physical, mental, emotional, and spiritual aspects – are intertwined and affect our well-being. The following stories demonstrate the aspects of lovematism and illustrate challenges where something needs to change and shift.

When you reflect deeply on your life and choices, the natural byproduct is the experience of introspection and self-discovery. You may go through a range of emotions, such as regret, nostalgia, and gratitude. Even though these emotions may be complex or uncomfortable, they can provide valuable insights and inspiration.

You will relate to each story as you read along because they depict common issues such as work stress and personal struggles. These stories are meant to make you reflect to help you grow personally by considering a more holistic approach. Think about how to apply the YOU value of the YEARN advantage.

TOM has been feeling stressed at work lately, affecting his physical health. He's been having trouble sleeping and skipping meals due to his workload. He realizes he must manage his stress better and starts practicing mindfulness meditation to improve his mental and emotional well-being. With regular meditation, Tom can calm his mind to reduce his anxiety. He also begins to feel more energized and focused, which helps him to be more productive at work. *These are the mind and emotional aspects.*

JOHN is going through a difficult time in his life. He's lost his job and feels lost and disconnected from his sense of purpose. He starts volunteering at a local charity organization to give back to the community and connect with something larger than himself. This helps him improve his emotional and spiritual well-being. Through his volunteer work, John can make a positive impact on others, which gives him a sense of purpose and fulfillment. He also finds that he feels more connected to a higher power or the importance of spirituality. *These are the emotional and spiritual aspects.*

LEILA has been stuck in her career and is looking for ways to improve her skills and learn new things. She enrolls in a continuing education program to improve her mental and intellectual well-being. She starts exercising regularly to improve her physical health. Through her continuing education program, Leila can expand her knowledge and skills. This enhances her confidence and sense of accomplishment. She also finds that exercise helps her feel more energized and reduces her stress. *These are the mental and physical aspects.*

JACK is going through a divorce and is struggling to manage his emotions. He decides to seek therapy to work on his emotional well-being and meditate to improve his mental and spiritual health. Through treatment, Jack can process his emotions and work through the challenges of his divorce. He also finds that meditation helps him to feel more centered and connected to his spirituality. *These are the mental, emotional, and spiritual aspects.*

SOFIA has always been interested in spirituality and wants to deepen her connection to something larger than herself. She starts practicing yoga and meditation to improve her spiritual well-being. She begins volunteering at a local charity organization to enhance her emotional well-being. Sofia can connect with her spirituality through yoga and meditation and find inner peace. She also finds that her volunteer work helps her feel more connected to her community and improves her empathy and compassion. *These are the physical, emotional, and spiritual aspects.*

MATIAS has been struggling with his physical health due to his sedentary lifestyle and poor diet. He decides to start exercising and eating healthier to improve his physical well-being. He also starts practicing mindfulness meditation to improve his mental and emotional well-being. With regular exercise and a more nutritious diet, Matias can improve his physical health and reduce his risk of chronic diseases. He also finds that meditation helps him to feel more relaxed and centered, which enhances his well-being. *These are the physical and mental aspects.*

LISA is going through a significant life transition and is feeling overwhelmed and anxious. She seeks therapy to work on her emotional and mental well-being and starts journaling to help process her thoughts and emotions. Through treatment, Lisa can work through her anxieties and develop coping strategies to manage her stress. She also finds that journaling helps her express and clarify her feelings. Lisa begins to explore her values and beliefs through meditation and reflection. This allows her to connect with her spirituality and improve her well-being. *These are the emotional, mental, and spiritual aspects.*

YOU - Define Your Motivation

The "You" core value of the YEARN Advantage focuses on understanding your motivators and goals. To define your motivation, consider the following questions:

Next Questions for 'YOU'

- ## Why do I want to do 'it' (what drives you)?
- ## Why do I want to achieve this goal(s)?

The letter Y is the first letter in YOU. The letter Y has a similar pronunciation to the word "WHY." *Why?* is a question that relates to your motivation, the underlying reasons for your actions.

Knowing your 'why' is part of your self-discovery. This does not identify the 'what' (we go over that in the next chapter). To discover more about yourself, focus on WHY. By defining your motivation, you will understand why you want to achieve your goal. This understanding will help you stay on track, motivated, and focused. You'll also be able to tap into your inner drive and determination to overcome obstacles that come your way.

For some people, if you remove their grievances, you take away their purpose for living. While hope serves as a positive source of nourishment for most people, there is a minority who derive psychological motivation from their negative issues. Without these negative emotions, they would feel lost and without direction in life. Certain people need a drill sergeant for a coach, not a cheerleader. Find which is your motivation and use it to excel.

Several vital components influence your behavior and the choices you make. These include: your attitude, which encompasses your thoughts and feelings about things, your expectations, hopes for what will happen, beliefs, and convictions about what is true or real. These all work together to determine the direction of your actions and interactions.

BELIEFS & MINDSET MATTER

It's no secret that having a positive outlook on life can make it easier to handle difficult situations. With a positive mindset, we're more likely to view our problems as opportunities for growth rather than obstacles to overcome. This helps us stay focused on the good things in our lives instead of feeling overwhelmed by the negatives.

Beliefs are both the mental and emotional aspects of lovematism. And, of course, there are spiritual beliefs.

You can change your attitude and beliefs by developing a positive and empowered mindset. This change can result in positive outcomes in your life. The ability to experience happiness lies within your own hands. By focusing on the present moment and avoiding negative thoughts, you can cultivate a positive state of mind to see new possibilities.

The opposite of an empowered mindset is a locked mindset. The mind stays in the lock position to maintain without accepting change, growth or embracing the new.

Self-discovery is a lifelong journey. Unlock your true potential with continual learning, exploration, and experimentation.

Although doctors, nutritionists, teachers, and trainers can give advice, we are ultimately responsible for our own mental and physical health, education, and personal development.

Our beliefs are primarily subconscious. Many factors may influence your beliefs, such as:

1. *Education:* The ideas and perspectives you're exposed to through education and experiences can influence your beliefs.
2. *Religion:* Religious beliefs and practices can affect your worldview and help you achieve inner peace.
3. *Media:* News and social media can impact your opinions by presenting detailed information.
4. *Life experiences:* Significant life events can impact your beliefs, such as successes, failures, or major transitions.
5. *Age and generational differences:* Different age groups may have different values and attitudes that shape their beliefs.
6. *Gender:* Societal expectations around gender can affect your attitudes and perspectives.
7. *Peer groups:* Your friends, colleagues, and social networks can influence your beliefs.
8. *Race and ethnicity:* Your racial and ethnic identity can impact your beliefs based on cultural values and experiences.
9. *Geography:* Your surroundings can influence your beliefs, thoughts, and actions.

10. *Language*: Your language and its cultural meanings can impact your beliefs and perceptions. The Sapir-Whorf hypothesis, also called linguistic relativity hypothesis, proposes that the language we use affects our thoughts, beliefs, and concepts about the world.

11. *Neurodiversity:* Conditions such as autism, ADHD, and dyslexia can affect one's sense of identity and their place in society. Being included or excluded and being accommodated properly can have a significant impact on how individuals navigate the world.

12. *Personality:* Traits such as openness to experience or neuroticism can influence your beliefs.

13. *Trauma*: Traumatic experiences like war or abuse can impact your beliefs.

14. *Historical context*: Historical events and trends transforming society and the world can bias your beliefs and political affiliations.

15. *Technology:* Technology and artificial intelligence can shape your experiences and interactions with the world, affecting your beliefs.

16. *Social class:* Your social class or economic status can determine your beliefs based on cultural norms and values associated with different financial systems.

These are just some of the factors that may influence your beliefs. Your beliefs comprise a complex interplay of individual, cultural, historical, and contextual factors. Understanding these influences can help you better understand why you hold the beliefs you do.

The experiences and outcomes you attract into your life reflect your inner self. This includes your thoughts, beliefs, emotions, and behaviors. The external reality you experience directly reflects your internal reality. We attract what we focus on, think about, and believe, manifesting in our lives in multiple ways.

For example, if you are feeling angry, you are more likely to perceive situations as unfavorable and feel more frustrated. If you are feeling happy and content, you are more likely to perceive situations as positive and feel more optimistic.

Your feelings toward yourself heavily influence your feelings toward other people. Developing positive relationships with others can be difficult if you do not have a positive or comfortable relationship with yourself. Many people go through life without realizing this fact. It can be challenging for some people to acknowledge that personal issues might cause their negative emotions or relationships, so they blame others. This can hinder their ability to fix the underlying problems and form better connections in relationships.

It starts with you. If you are comfortable with yourself, you are more likely to be accepting of others and their differences. Self-comfort is a crucial factor in developing positive relationships with others. You are more likely to be empathetic, kind, and understanding, which can lead to positive and meaningful relationships. What if you are not comfortable with yourself? Then you may project your doubts onto others, which can hinder your ability to address the underlying issues that affect your ability to form positive relationships with others. You may be judgmental and defensive or create barriers to positive relationships.

To believe in yourself, you must cultivate an empowered mindset of openness and self-affirmation. Seek out and focus on thoughts that reinforce your confidence, competence, and self-worth. You may need help to focus on these thoughts long enough to allow them to take root and become a consistent part of your self-concept. An empowered mindset sees opportunities to grow.

Are you someone who feels the way to attain your ambitions in life is by focusing on your 'inner being' or your 'inner self' but you are struggling? It may be that your struggle is because you are working hard externally and this does not fit with your flow. You might be tempted to stick to the path of working hard, but eventually, you'll realize that this approach alone may not be right for your flow. It's important to take some time to look within yourself. Activate your 'inner being' so you can advance faster than you ever envisioned toward a rewarding and successful life.

Only some people are deeply connected with the fourth aspect of lovematism, the spiritual aspect. Not everyone has this feeling of a deep inner journey. You can devote yourself to your soul path to genuine and enduring joy, success, and inner harmony.

For those who don't have the inner journey drive, you can use focus and effort as the key to success. It is not a narrow path; you can be on a combined path. It is up to you which paths you take to reach your goals and achieve greatness.

We can affect our experiences and outcomes by working on our internal state, thoughts, beliefs, and emotions. If we cultivate a strong and positive mindset, we can attract favorable people and experiences and achieve what we desire.

Life is not always easy, and hardships can often be catalysts. Throughout history, many people have overcome significant obstacles and adversity and accomplish amazing feats of greatness.

Here are two examples of two famous ladies who have overcome adversity and achieved distinction:

One example is Oprah Winfrey, the entrepreneur, media mogul, and philanthropist. Raised in poverty, she made something of her life despite a childhood full of hardship. She has become one of the world's most influential women and an inspiration to many people around the globe.

Another example is JK Rowling, the author of the Harry Potter series. In her early adult years, after facing financial difficulties and dealing with depression, Rowling went on to write one of the most successful book series in history. Her story is a remarkable testament to how much can be accomplished when facing obstacles head-on.

Affirmation for YOU:

I am worth investing in myself.

The self-transformation journey begins when we challenge our thinking and confront limiting beliefs and narratives.

Question your thoughts and beliefs and challenge the assumptions that have defined you. This process of introspection and self-examination can be uncomfortable. It is necessary to break free from the constraints of your own mental frameworks. Being open to new perspectives and ideas can expand your understanding of yourself and the world around you. This creates the possibility for growth, transformation, and a better version of yourself.

The Struggle to FOCUS

It can be difficult to focus on positive thoughts about ourselves for long enough to make them stick. There are a couple of reasons for this. Our brains have a natural negativity bias, meaning we tend to pay more attention to negative experiences and thoughts than positive ones. This bias helped our ancestors to survive in dangerous environments by quickly identifying potential threats and harm. In modern life, this bias can make it difficult to focus on positive self-affirmations and overlook our strengths and accomplishments.

Some distractions can make it challenging to focus on ourselves intentionally. Today's fast-paced and technology-driven world provides numerous distractions that can make it hard to carve out the necessary time and mental space to focus on our positive qualities. These factors can make it tough to concentrate on positive self-affirmations, but it is important to persevere and consciously cultivate an empowered mindset. Properly value your environment to support yourself sufficiently. This will be reviewed in the E core value.

To overcome the challenge of focusing on positive self-affirmations, there are several steps you can take. Practicing mindfulness, setting aside dedicated time for self-reflection and positive self-talk, seeking support from others, and learning to identify and challenge negative self-talk are some strategies you can use. Prioritizing your mental and emotional well-being by intentionally focusing on positive self-affirmations can strengthen your belief in yourself and improve your quality of life.

Todd Herman works with many high-achievers. In his book, "The Alter Ego Effect," he introduces the concept of using an alter ego as a coaching tool to overcome mental barriers and achieve one's goals. The book presents scientific research and offers examples of how changing alter egos can be used in specific situations. Herman emphasizes the importance of integrating your alter ego into your everyday life for long-term development.

The struggle to focus affects high achievers, too. It can be daunting for high achievers to contemplate dealing with their emotional traumas, as they may fear it will detract from their edge. Tackling these issues can boost their inborn talents without compromising their strengths. Healing can augment a high achiever's inherent skills rather than let past hurts hold them back.

Successful people who have faced and healed emotional distress rarely regress or fail. Many high achievers have found greater success and contentment in their personal and professional lives once they deal with emotional distress.

Have a look at the traits of high achievers who consistently achieve their dreams and rise to greatness despite setbacks and challenges:

1. FOCUS: To be highly focused and use their time wisely on their most important goals. They prioritize their time and energy

toward achieving their goals and are not easily distracted by other things.

2. PERSEVERANCE: Are willing to put in the hard work and effort required to achieve their goals. They understand that success often requires long hours, dedication, and sacrifice.

3. RESILIENCE: To bounce back from failures and setbacks quickly. They view these setbacks as opportunities for growth and learning rather than reasons to give up.

4. ADAPTABILITY: Can adapt to changing circumstances and adjust their plans as needed. They are not rigid in their thinking and are willing to pivot if necessary.

5. POSITIVE MINDSET: Use an empowered, positive mindset and often use visualization. They believe in their ability to succeed and are not deterred by setbacks or negative feedback.

Which of these five traits do YOU regularly practice in your life?

To move forward and live in the present, it's crucial to recognize and overcome emotional and psychological barriers. By letting go of grudges, prejudices, and fears, we can grow personally and contribute to societal progress, which can create a better future.

YOU and How You See the World

"It's not what you look at that matters;
it's what you see."
~Henry David Thoreau

Your being, or the essence of who you are, reflects your level of understanding and knowledge. The more you learn and understand about the world, the better your actions and decisions will be.

It is essential to constantly challenge yourself and expand your understanding of various topics and perspectives. By doing so, you will develop a more well-rounded and informed perspective, which will enhance the quality of your being.

Think carefully about the information you find, challenge assumptions and biases, and consider different viewpoints. This can help you develop critical thinking skills and make informed decisions while avoiding misinformation. As you continue to improve these skills, you can better handle complicated problems and communicate more efficiently with others.

YOU and Ambition

Napoleon Bonaparte once said, *"Great ambition is central to great potential."* This statement holds true for you as well. Depending on personal guiding principles, ambitious individuals may act ethically or unethically.

Great ambition can be a powerful force that drives your potential. It motivates you to set high goals and work hard to achieve them. Your intense desire to accomplish something can fuel your efforts and help you achieve levels of success that may have seemed impossible before.

With great ambition, you can push yourself outside your comfort zone, take risks, and learn new skills or knowledge to pursue your goals. Embracing challenges and overcoming obstacles can help you develop important qualities like resilience and perseverance, two essential qualities for realizing your full potential.

Ambition alone does not guarantee greatness. You must possess the necessary skills, abilities, and resources. You must be willing to learn from mistakes, and be open to feedback to achieve greatness. Great ambition can be powerful, motivating you to set high goals, take risks, and develop resilience and perseverance.

Channel your ambition on goals or activities that align with your passions and values. This can bring a sense of purpose and fulfillment, motivating and driving you toward success.

YOU and Personal Agency

When looking at your life story, your personal agency, context, and narrative are deeply connected. Personal agency refers to your ability to make decisions and take actions that shape your life's direction and experiences. The narrative of your life story is a result of how you have navigated your context and put your personal agency into action. Your choices and actions form the course of your life and experiences. Your life story's narrative also reflects your values and the significance you attach to specific events.

Crafting your life story involves taking control of your life by making choices and acting on them based on your values and aspirations, which can bring a sense of satisfaction. It's essential to acknowledge that your actions, context, circumstances, and environment, such as your family, society, culture, and economic status, are components of your life story. Taking ownership of your choices and actions can help you make the most of your context while writing your life story in a meaningful way.

Narrative identity, the narrative you design about yourself, includes people you consider heroes and villains, memorable moments, challenges you have faced, and your struggles. When expressing yourself to others, you share your story; when wanting to know more about someone, you ask them about their story. Your life story is not just a collection of everything that has happened to you. You choose which events to focus on and emphasize, both positive and negative, that have shaped you and helped you understand your experiences. How you interpret these events can be different for everyone.

When contemplating your story's central theme, exciting patterns appear. Dan McAdams, a psychologist from Northwestern University, discovered that individuals desire to contribute to society and often construct redemptive stories when reflecting on their lives. Even traumatic experiences can be valuable lessons in resilience, while difficult circumstances can bring individuals closer to their families. For example, caring for a terminally ill friend may inspire someone to prioritize their relationships with loved ones.

Stories can provide purpose and don't end with simply writing the tale. The stories you create about yourself can motivate you to take meaningful actions, such as dedicating time to an important cause. Sharing your story can also help you live up to it. Modifying your narrative allows you to form a positive identity that motivates you toward your goals. People who think their lives are meaningful often tell stories about growth, connection, and personal agency. Stories allow you to build a positive identity where you are in control, feel loved, and progress in life no matter the difficulties.

Where are YOU now?

Have you ever felt like you're living in the past, even though you're in the present day, with access to technology and advanced knowledge?

"Psychological time" means our past experiences, beliefs, and emotions can change how we see time, which may not be the same as reality. People who hold on to historical grudges, prejudices, and fears are stuck in the past, which may not be helpful in today's society. Sadly, a few people come to mind as I write these words. Nothing can seem to budge them; they hold firmly to their grudge.

We live in the present, but our psychological time may still be stuck in a bygone era. This prevents us from progressing as individuals and in society.

Grudges are long-held resentments or grievances arising from past conflicts or injustices. These grudges can prevent you or groups from progressing, leading to ongoing tensions and conflicts. Similarly, prejudices may be obsolete and appear as attitudes or beliefs many people hold even though they are no longer relevant or accurate. History is full of war and genocide based on prejudice and assumption of superiority. These prejudices can manifest as racism, sexism, homophobia, and other forms of discrimination. Prejudice prevents individuals from fully participating in society.

Deep down, there may be hidden fears that are the unconscious or subconscious fears that can control our behavior and decisions.

Many fears and struggles in our society are not life-threatening, that put you in physical danger. The psychological, inner fear of insecurity and destructive patterns does not serve you. Fear that originates from past traumas or negative experiences can continue to impact your thoughts and actions if not addressed. Remain conscious and keep your heart open and release your fear.

YOU and Failure: A Prerequisite for Greatness

Making mistakes and failing are common experiences that can be discouraging and demotivating. **Failure is not a barrier but a prerequisite to greatness.** Failure teaches us valuable lessons and provides us with feedback to help us improve.

Many successful people have experienced numerous failures before achieving greatness. These failures often provide the necessary lessons and experiences to help them reach their goals. For example, it is said Thomas Edison failed over 1,000 times before inventing the light bulb. Each failure taught him something new and helped him improve his design until he finally achieved success.

Here are more examples of successful people who faced failure before achieving greatness:

- Michael Jordan, widely considered one of the greatest basketball players of all time, was cut from his high school basketball team.
- Albert Einstein, the renowned physicist, failed his Swiss Federal Polytechnic School entrance exam.
- Steven Spielberg, one of the most successful film directors of all time, was rejected from film school multiple times.
- Walt Disney, the creator of Mickey Mouse and founder of Disney, was fired from a newspaper for lacking creativity and imagination.
- Vincent van Gogh, the post-impressionist painter, only sold one painting during his lifetime and struggled with mental illness.
- Abraham Lincoln, the 16th President of the United States, experienced many failures in his personal and professional life, including multiple election losses, before being elected President.
- Stephen King, the best-selling author of horror and suspense novels, had his first novel rejected by publishers 30 times before it was accepted for publication.
- Colonel Sanders, the founder of Kentucky Fried Chicken, was rejected over 1,000 times before finding a restaurant willing to franchise his recipe.

Perfection isn't attainable; wishing for perfection can result in satisfaction and burnout. Taking responsibility for one's actions and decisions shows maturity, leadership, and integrity.

At times, we experience brief moments of insight that enhance our clarity of vision, making it easier to make better decisions. Maturity helps make it easier to make improved decisions in the moment.

Greatness does not mean being error-free. Greatness is about owning up to your mistakes and utilizing them as chances to gain knowledge and enhance oneself. Being responsible, rather than perfect, is an attribute of greatness.

Universal, Timeless Principles

Developing yourself is a continuous journey. It's about honing your personality and leveraging your strengths while addressing any weaknesses. It's a challenge, but with the right attitude, anyone can make headway on their path to becoming the best version of themselves.

At the heart of self-improvement are universal, timeless principles. These can be applied in any situation, regardless of time, culture, or context. A few of these widely accepted truths include:

Attitude: Going the extra mile with a smile, being a beacon of positivity, and having a grateful mindset. Have the courage to make tough decisions when necessary.

Discipline: Achieving goals requires managing your thoughts, actions, and emotions. It means setting clear objectives and consistently following through to make them happen. Success in financial matters, relationships, and personal development requires discipline. With practice, you can achieve whatever you strive for.

Responsibility & Honesty: Taking ownership means being accountable for your decisions not blaming others. Be honest and truthful with yourself and others and be responsible for your life.

Integrity: Being trustworthy and consistent in your values and actions, even when no one is watching or there is no immediate reward or punishment.

Respect: Respect the worth and dignity of all people.

Fairness: Treating everyone equally and without prejudice.

Human Dignity: Believing each person has value and should be treated with kindness and consideration.

Service: Dedication for the benefit of others and the greater good.

By putting these principles into practice, you'll progress on your self-improvement journey. This is a repetitive theme.

> ***"The only person you are destined to become***
> ***is the person you decide to be."***
> ~Ralph Waldo Emerson

The "Volume" of YOU:

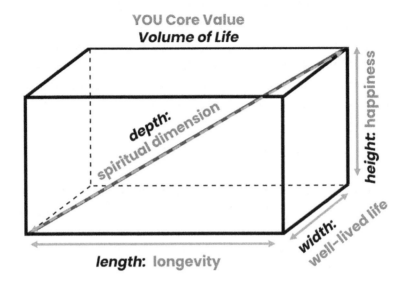

Figure 1 YOU Core Value in Volume

Envision the YOU core values of life as a four-dimensional space. Each dimension represents an essential aspect of the human experience.

Longevity of Life (length) is the amount of time one lives. However, longevity alone is insufficient to make a fulfilling or meaningful life.

Well-lived life (width) encompasses relationships, career, education, experiences, and more. It is affected by social connections, financial stability, physical health, and mental well-being.

Happiness in Life (height) represents the degree of satisfaction and contentment you experience in life. Happiness is an essential component of a fulfilling life. To live a happy and fulfilling life prioritize what matters to you. Take wise actions and strive toward achieving your personal goals and aspirations.

Spiritual Dimension (depth) brings a sense of purpose, meaning, and connection to something beyond oneself. It includes religion, meditation, mindfulness, self-reflection, and inner exploration. Spirituality may be a source of comfort, hope, and resilience during challenging times. Spirituality exists even if you are an atheist.

When you consider all four dimensions, you maximize the "volume" of life. Each YOU dimension is interconnected and contributes to the quality of life. A life well-lived is filled with feelings of happiness, personal achievement, and spiritual connection.

Here are a few tips for YOU - Your self-improvement:

To believe in yourself, you must cultivate an empowered mindset of self-affirmation. Actively seek out and focus on thoughts that reinforce your confidence, competence, and self-worth.

Identify Your Goals: Take the time to think about what you want to achieve. Set realistic goals and figure out ways to work on them. Visualize what success looks like and strive to make your dreams a reality. Jump into the *Activate Enhavim* section to learn more.

Vision and Purpose: Establish a clear vision and purpose to direct your decisions and actions. These values will guide you toward self-improvement. See more in the *Activate Enhavim* section.

Focus on Your Strengths: Think about the skills you already have and look for ways to sharpen them. This will help to increase your confidence and resilience.

Address Your Weaknesses: Acknowledge any areas of weakness and set goals to work on them. Stretch a bit further than you think you can and take action to make improvements.

Proactivity and Control: Take the initiative and take action and direction of your life.

Please focus on what matters: Life can be overwhelming, and getting lost in small details is easy. Prioritize what matters, like relationships, values, and goals, to keep on track.

Be willing to be seen as imperfect: Accepting our faults and mistakes is essential to self-improvement. Open up to constructive criticism and feedback and use it as a learning opportunity.

Be Joyful: Find joy in the little things and be grateful for the blessings in your life. Gratitude. This is the key to a fulfilling life.

Learn, Learn, and Learn: Never stop learning. Develop new skills through formal education, online courses, or self-study. This will enable you to grow and become a well-rounded individual.

Learn to Confront and Initiate Change: Get out of your comfort zone. Change can be intimidating, but it's an essential life skill that will help you grow.

Change example: The Covid-19 pandemic challenged the traditional classroom concept, leading to a re-evaluation of teaching methods. Simply imparting information is now done easily online and with

AI-generated text responses. Teachers must inspire curiosity in their students. This creates lifelong learners who seek knowledge and personal growth beyond formal education.

Live in the Now: Seize the day and be present in your life. Embrace risks, get out of your comfort zone, and take advantage of opportunities that come your way.

Personal Self-Care: Practice mindfulness, physical exercise, and relax to show yourself some self-love. Take care of all four aspects of lovematism: body, mind, heart, soul.

Create your legacy daily. *"It takes 20 years to build a reputation and five minutes to ruin it. If you think about that, you'll do things differently."* ~Warren Buffett

Remember, self-improvement is a continuous process. Keep working towards your goals, learn from your failures and successes, and don't be afraid to seek help when needed.

REVIEW Questions for 'YOU'

- # Who are You?
- # What is your Identity?
- # Why do I want to do 'it' (what drives you)?
- # Why do I want to achieve this goal(s)?

E - Where does it take Place?

"Be careful the environment you choose, for it will shape you; be careful the friends you choose, for you will become like them."

~W. Clement Stone

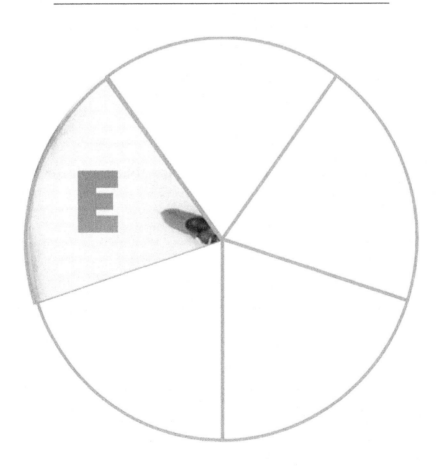

ENVIRONMENT (PLACE)
IS CORE VALUE #2

"Eencourage and nurture a space that motivates and energizes greatness!"

ENVIRONMENT

⇨ Have you set up the right surroundings? What KEY FACTORS contribute to a supportive or draining ENVIRONMENT? How can you make necessary changes?

The 'Environment' core value of the YEARN Advantage focuses on the physical and digital spaces you occupy. To set up the right surroundings, consider the following questions:

• Where is this goal to take place?

• What physical spaces will support me in achieving this goal?

- What digital spaces will support me in achieving this goal?

- What distractions in my environment may hinder me?

When you set up the right surroundings, you create an environment that supports your goals, enhances your focus and concentration, and makes growth more manageable.

Our environment refers to the various settings and contexts in which we live and operate. These environments can significantly impact our well-being, behaviors, and choices.

Our environment includes physical, social, and cultural factors which significantly impacts our beliefs and attitudes, affecting our overall well-being. Creating a supportive environment that aligns with your goals is essential for growth and success.

A healthy and conducive physical environment fosters creativity, productivity, and well-being. Intentionally modifying your environment can lead to positive changes in behavior and attitude. Positive habits and practices that align with goals can help create a supportive environment.

Surrounding oneself with people who inspire, support, and challenge you can help you become the person you want to be. Environment can affect one's mindset, motivation, and self-esteem.

Question for 'ENVIRONMENT'

- **Where do you want to be?**

MAJOR ENVIRONMENTS

The built environment: The human-made structures and spaces where we live, work, and play. This includes homes, offices, public buildings, and urban spaces.

The physical and natural environment: The natural world around us. Forests, oceans, and mountains, as well as sub-atomic particles, the planets, and the universe.

Note: The physics of quantum mechanics teaches us about two discoveries. First, quarks are tiny particles that form atoms and have two unique traits: observing them alters them, and they can exist in two places at once. Second, our perspective creates our reality on a quantum level. What we see depends on where we stand and our perspective, and that determines what comes into being. When we observe an event in our environment, it alters the event. This shows that our perspective affects our objective reality by changing our viewpoint. Physicists propose that we are not distinct from our environment. We impact reality as if we are a single organism functioning as a whole; we are in unison with the environment.

"For most people, we often marvel at the beauty of a sunrise or the magnificence of a full moon, but it is impossible to fathom the magnitude of the universe that surrounds us."
~Richard Baker

The digital environment: Online spaces and technologies are increasingly integral to our daily lives. Social media platforms, online marketplaces, virtual reality, artificial intelligence, and a myriad of digital communication tools.

The economic environment: The economic systems and structures that shape our lives. Financial markets and institutions, employment opportunities, and currency. It also includes factors such as income inequality, access to resources, and the availability of social safety nets. *This will be reviewed in the R core value.*

The cultural environment: The shared beliefs, values, and practices in our society and communities. It encompasses art, music, literature, religion, and other aspects of culture. The culture factors that influence our perceptions and behaviors. This also relates to YOU and your RELATIONSHIPS. *This will be reviewed in the N core value.*

These various environments can significantly impact our physical, mental, emotional, and even our spiritual well-being. Understanding how environment forms our lives is essential for creating healthier and more sustainable communities.

Let's delve deeper into these environments:

A. The Built Environment:

The built environment is where we live, work, and play. It includes everything from skyscrapers and neighborhoods to public buildings and parks. It's a testament to our ingenuity and creativity.

Look at a cityscape - it is an impressive example of the built environment created by humans for our living, working, and leisure. It started with an idea and grew from an enhavim (see more in the *Activate Enhavim* section later in the book).

Our built environment comprises the structures we inhabit, the objects we use, the clothes we wear, and the spaces we occupy. It includes the complex network of roads, bridges, and buildings. The space we live and work in significantly impacts our mindset and productivity.

A cityscape can be a striking example of the built environment. Tall buildings and complex roads symbolize human-made spaces. This is the physical world crafted by human hands and minds, providing us with our places and spaces.

Our homes, workplaces, parks, playgrounds, and shopping malls can shape the physical world and our social lives. It provides access to resources and services that support our daily lives.

Our built environment can be used as a tool for social justice, giving individuals a chance to be part of their communities. For example, providing accessible public transportation or creating affordable housing can help create an equitable society.

The built environment can also affect our mental and physical well-being. By creating places that are accessible and inviting, we can foster a sense of belonging and connection. This involves creating spaces where people can come together and can participate in activities that encourage physical movement and exercise. For example, having places to walk and bike and green areas to relax can help people stay healthy and connected to their communities. Creating safe, secure, and accessible spaces can reduce stress and anxiety.

It's important to consider how the design of our physical spaces can impact our lives and our communities. Investing in our built environment with a holistic approach to urban design can help us create inviting, equitable, and vibrant places.

Our infrastructure and technology are constantly changing. Technology allows us to connect with our surroundings in new ways and interact with people worldwide. Our physical spaces continually evolve to meet today's needs and into the future.

Objects in the built environment: Objects in our space can also have memory associations. If something in our environment has a negative memory associated with it, it can affect our mood and mindset. For example, a broken object in our space can constantly remind us of our failure to fix it. If possible, fix or give away such objects and focus on things that bring positivity and good memories.

An organized, clean environment can help us feel more relaxed, focused, and productive. If our environment is cluttered and disorganized, it can affect our ability to focus, concentrate, and be productive. Similarly, the clothes we wear can also affect our mindset and productivity. Dressing professionally for work, for example, can help us feel more confident and competent. Your mind and body will thank you for it! It is crucial to take the time to declutter and organize our surroundings, whether it's at home or work.

You can free up resources for what's important by making your living space less cluttered, prioritizing commitments aligned with your goals, and ending toxic relationships. This intentional decluttering can lead to a more fulfilling and purposeful life, where you can focus on what brings joy and adds value to your life.

Viktor Frankl was an Austrian neurologist, psychiatrist, Holocaust survivor, and author of the famous book: *Man's Search for Meaning.* Frankl believed that *although humans cannot control their external circumstances or their environment,* they have the freedom to choose their attitudes and responses to the circumstances that arise within those environments. He argued that even in extreme situations, like the Holocaust concentration camps, individuals still have the power to choose their response, which can impact their mental and emotional well-being.

The freedom to choose is not just a matter of individual choice but also a sense of responsibility and commitment to others. Frankl believed humans are responsible for contributing to the world and making it a better place. This sense of purpose and meaning is essential for human well-being. His concept of freedom and power to choose underscores the importance of individuals taking an active role in shaping their lives and finding meaning, even when facing difficult circumstances.

Our built environment significantly impacts our daily lives, including our mindset, productivity, and well-being.

B. The Physical and Natural Environment:

The physical and natural environment are the natural wonders and human-made structures that encompass our communities. Built resources like airplanes, cars, boats, and roads allow us to connect to the mountains and forests that define our landscapes. We can thrive in the physical and natural environment that is an ever-evolving tapestry of beauty and innovation. Many people feel a connection to a higher power in nature.

Nature is an environment we interact with daily, whether we realize it or not. Spending time in nature positively impacts our creativity and mental health. Unfortunately, many of us have our days cooped up inside, breathing recycled air and under fluorescent lights. It's essential to connect with nature. Experience outdoor activities like hiking, surfing, snowboarding, or simply take a walk outside during the day. Even breathing fresh air can help clear your mind and boost your mood.

Incorporating nature into our work lives can also be beneficial. Walk-and-talk meetings have been shown to increase creativity and productivity. Many successful people like Mark Zuckerberg and the late Steve Jobs have been known to conduct walking meetings. If you don't have access to outdoor spaces, add plants to your workspace. This is a simple way to bring a bit of nature indoors and create a more natural environment. Plants can help improve air quality, reduce stress, and boost productivity and creativity.

Forests are the most crucial natural environment on the planet. They provide essential habitats for many species of plants and animals, as well as clean air and water. Forests are also home to countless species of birds, mammals, reptiles, amphibians, insects, and fish. Forests provide us with renewable resources such as lumber and fuel wood. Trees are essential to maintaining the balance of our ecosystem. Trees absorb carbon dioxide from the atmosphere and provide a habitat and food for numerous species.

Oceans cover nearly three-quarters of the Earth's surface and are home to a myriad of life forms. From coral reefs to deep-sea trenches, oceans provide habitats for incredible species diversity.

Mountains have existed since the beginning of time and are awe-inspiring landscapes today. They can range from small hills to massive ranges that stretch across continents. Mountains provide a variety of habitats for animals and plants, which have adapted over time to live in these harsh environments. Mountains represent some spiritual significance to many cultures throughout the world.

We can look up at night and be amazed by the beauty of our universe. From planets to galaxies; stars to comets; black holes to asteroids; there is so much out there that we can never fully comprehend it all! The universe is full of mystery and wonder that will keep us learning forever.

C. The Digital Environment:

The digital environment is the world of online spaces and technologies that are integral to our daily lives. It includes e-commerce marketplaces, social media platforms, and other online spaces that connect us around the world. There's a constantly evolving landscape of innovation and connectivity which offers endless possibilities for exploration and discovery.

Many people use social media to connect with friends, family, and colleagues. We can also use it to find new communities or explore interests in different ways. We may use websites to find information on various topics or to keep up with current events.

Technology has revolutionized the way we conduct business and interact with each other. Digital communication tools have made it easier for people to stay in touch regardless of location. Email, text messaging, and video conferencing are just a few of the tech tools available. This has also made remote work more accessible and enabled people to access services like banking and shopping from the comfort of their homes.

The growth of technology has allowed us to stay connected more than ever before. Here are some technology benefits:

- Increased efficiency in communication
- The ability to access resources quickly
- Convenience in conducting transactions
- Enhanced security for personal data
- Improved accuracy of information shared

Our online presence and social networks significantly impact our lives in this digital age. Social media platforms like Facebook, Twitter, Instagram, Discord, YouTube and LinkedIn offer us the chance to connect. We can share ideas with individuals from diverse backgrounds and cultures and collaborate on projects. These networks create a digital environment for us to interact in and help shape the relationships we build and maintain.

Remember, we have the power to curate our online presence and networks. Invest in creating a robust online profile. This can help maximize opportunities on social media platforms, whether by connecting with industry professionals, following thought leaders and influencers, or engaging in online communities for growth and opportunities. Artificial intelligence adds a whole other layer.

It's essential to use these networks wisely and be mindful of their impact on our mental health and well-being. It's easy to fall into the trap of social comparison, where we constantly compare ourselves to others and feel inadequate. It is essential to balance our online activities with real-life experiences and interactions.

Online environments have become an integral part of our lives, and embracing and using them in ways that benefit us is crucial. Be selective with your online connections. Create positive interactions and balance your online presence with real-life experiences. Your digital environment should promote personal development, and foster meaningful relationships.

Each age group has different online usage. Various sources indicate that Millennials are heavy internet users, spending an average of 7.2 hours per day online. They frequently use the shop online using their mobile devices and actively seek out coupons. They average 2.4 hours per day watching online videos, and on social media, an average of 2 hours and 38 minutes per day.

Our online presence and participation in digital networks significantly impact our lives. Tt's essential to wisely balance our online activities with real-life experiences to safeguard our mental health and well-being.

1. *Social networks:* Networks allow users to create profiles, connect with others, and share content.

2. *Messaging platforms:* Platforms allow users to communicate with each other through private messages or group chats. Examples include WhatsApp, Telegram, and Discord.

3. *Online marketplaces* connect buyers and sellers of products and services. Examples include Amazon, eBay, and Etsy.

4. *Educational platforms:* Platforms provide online learning opportunities, such as massive open online courses (MOOCs), virtual classrooms, online tutorials, and short videos such as TED Talks. Examples include Coursera, edX, Masterclass, and Khan Academy.

5. *Entertainment platforms*: Platforms provide various forms of entertainment, such as music streaming services like Spotify and Pandora, video sharing platforms like YouTube and Vimeo, and gaming platforms like Steam and Twitch.

6. *News and information platforms:* Platforms provide news and information on various topics, such as current events, politics,

science, and technology. Examples include CNN, BBC, and Reddit.

7. *Professional networks*: Platforms connect professionals in various industries and provide opportunities for networking, job searching, and career development. Examples include LinkedIn and AngelList.

8. *AI and VR platforms:* Platforms are the way of the future for artificial intelligence to help create text content, images, and video content, and virtual reality for gaming and simulations.

These are just a few examples of the types of online environments that people interact with every day. Online environments continue to expand and evolve as the internet becomes more pervasive.

In our modern world, we become immersed in online environments which bombard our screens. These networks allow us to connect with people from all over the world, share ideas, and collaborate on projects.

With the internet, we can shape our network and build relationships with people who share our interests and values. Investing time in building and curating your online presence and networks is worth it to maximize opportunities. These online networks create a digital environment for us to interact and help shape the relationships we build and maintain.

Be cognizant that, as individuals, we have the power to curate our online presence. Building a solid online profile is takes considerable effort. Whether we connect with professionals, follow influencers, or engage in online communities, these platforms offer numerous opportunities.

Online environments have become an integral part of our lives. We can build a positive digital environment by carefully selecting our networks, engaging positively, and embracing the digital domain in ways that benefit both our online and real-life experiences.

Technology and the digital world have allowed us to create a global network that grows and becomes more interconnected every day.

In the Zoom era, many have built nicely lit prisons of thought in their offices, says my friend, James Kemp. Your current environment may keep you stuck in a loop. You may need to change it up.

Getting out of these places is essential to expand thinking and perspective. The more sensitive you are, the more you can utilize your environment to drive change. Try sitting in a new place and seeing things in a fresh environment. Sensitivity means you are especially sensitive to your surroundings. Move. Change. Shake it up. Let new ideas and perspectives flow out of your beautiful brain and soul.

How much time have you invested on a device connected to the internet today?

D. The Economic Environment:

The economic environment is crucial to our society, transforming our opportunities and challenges. It includes global markets, financial institutions, access to resources, and other assets. The availability of social safety nets such as welfare can provide help for those in need, giving everyone has a chance to succeed. *This will be reviewed in the R core value.*

E. The Cultural Environment:

The cultural environment is a diverse mix of shared beliefs, values, and practices. Culture influences our interactions with others and our worldview, from art, music, and literature to religion. Understanding our cultural environment can help build empathy and connection with others.

As we navigate the cultural environment, we can better understand ourselves and the world around us. We can foster empathy and connection with others. *This will be reviewed in the N core value.*

Note: Cultural and transgenerational epigenetic inheritance refers to the transmission of epigenetic gene changes across generations. Environmental epigenetics studies how genetic factors from previous generations affect gene expression.

'Artificial' and 'Regular' Environments

Have you ever attended a training seminar and felt a surge of motivation due to the supportive, new environment? What happens when you return to your 'regular' environment?

In an 'artificial' environment there is often an increase in motivation. This may be because of the positive and supportive environment, the novelty of the experience, meeting new people, and a strong emphasis on learning. It is common for this motivation to fade once we return to our 'regular' environment. It can be challenging to sustain the motivation gained in the 'artificial' environment.

Break down big tasks into smaller, achievable steps and schedule them to stay motivated in any environment. (We'll talk more about action steps in the next section of the YEARN Advantage.)

You already know that maintaining motivation is about more than just task planning and scheduling. The environment also plays a crucial role in nurturing motivation. A positive environment boosts motivation, while a hostile or unsupportive environment hinders motivation.

It is wise to surround yourself with supportive peers or mentors, set achievable goals, and celebrate small successes to maintain motivation even in the most challenging of environments.

Change the Scenery

Humanity cannot explore the vast expanse of space unless we have the courage to leave the safety and familiarity of Earth's surface.

To be constantly in the same environment, surrounded by the same people and things, can make you feel stagnant. Our brains become accustomed to the same stimuli directly wired into our subconscious. This may lead to a lack of motivation and energy, making it difficult to be productive and creative. It may require a change of scenery to disrupt the situation.

When we change our surroundings, even if it's just for a short time, we expose ourselves to new stimuli and experiences. This can stimulate our brains and help us to think in new ways. It can provide us with a fresh perspective and allow us to see things in a different light.

Take a break by going for a walk in a new neighborhood or taking a weekend trip to a nearby town. Change your surroundings to refresh your mind and body, increase productivity and creativity, and alter your mental state and attitude.

REVIEW Question for 'ENVIRONMENT'

- **Where do you want to be?**

A - When does Action happen?

"Success is not final; failure is not fatal: it is the courage to continue (to Act) that counts."
~ Winston Churchill

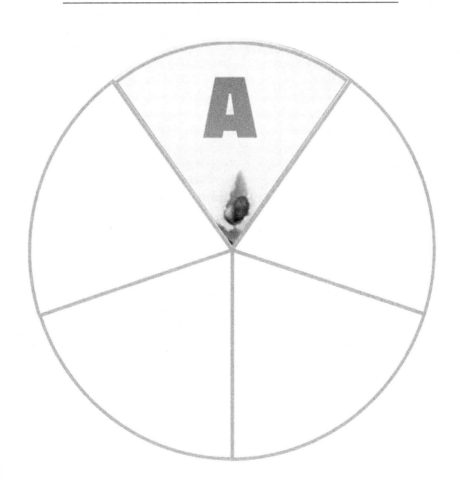

ACT (TAKE ACTION)
IS CORE VALUE #3

"A CT now and make it happen - Build the bridge between goals and greatness!"

Creating the bridge between your goals and greatness means clearly understanding what you want to achieve. Achieving greatness requires setting achievable goals and taking the necessary steps. It is crucial to recognize your unique qualities and how they can contribute to your success.

Everyone has different skills, interests, and strengths, so use yours in your favor! Identify what drives you and any obstacles that may stand in your way. Once you've set your sights on the success you want, take some time to plan out how you're going to get there. Set measurable objectives and establish a timeline for each one. Please ensure they are realistic and attainable so you don't become overwhelmed or discouraged. With that done, all that's left is to take action every day until you reach your goal. With hard work and dedication, success is within reach!

Question for 'ACT'

- **What do you want to do?**

A - What are the most CRUCIAL DECISIONS or ACTIONS you've taken in your life, and what motivated you to take them?

The "Act" core value defines short-term and long-term goals and activities to help you achieve your objectives; what you want to do. Short-term goals are the immediate steps towards progress. Long-term goals provide direction and purpose for your enhavim.

To define your short-term and long-term goals and actions, consider the following questions:

- What immediate steps must I take to achieve my goal?

- What steps must I take in the next few months to reach my goal?

- What do I need to achieve in the next year to get closer to my goal?

- What are my long-term goals for this objective, and what actions do I need to take to get there?

Defining short-term and long-term goals creates a clear roadmap with steps needed to achieve objectives in the near and far future. This approach helps you stay focused, motivated, and on track toward your goal.

Jim Rohn *says, "Your life only gets better when you do. Work on yourself, and the rest will follow."*

You can modify your life in the future. Recall the wise words of Mark Twain (Samuel Clemens), humorist, essayist, and novelist:

"Twenty years from now, you will be more disappointed by the things you didn't do than the ones you did."

The "things" you act upon or don't act upon create CHANGE.

Change is tricky. There are conflicting feelings when it comes to change. On the one hand, you may resist change because it disrupts your sense of stability and familiarity. Change can be uncomfortable and challenge your existing assumptions and habits. As such, you may prefer to maintain the status quo, even if it is not perfect.

On the other hand, you also desire to make progress in your life. The driving force behind why we seek change in areas like relationships, careers, or society is improvement. On a large scale, it's the advancement of humanity.

In any given situation, we always have three choices: we can either change it, accept it, or leave it behind.

The dilemma is that you want to change and things to remain the same. You want the benefits of change without the discomfort or disruption that it can bring. This creates tension between the desire for stability and progress, making it difficult to know how to move forward. Stability creates a sense of security and consistency, which can be crucial during uncertain or disruptive times. It would be best if you found a balance between these conflicting feelings.

Personal development is improving oneself through self-awareness, reflection, and intentional action. Without action, nothing changes.

You must embrace change, when necessary, even if it is uncomfortable or challenging. Find a balance to meet the challenges of change and achieve the desired progress and improvement. Continuity allows us to maintain the things that are important to us, such as our relationships, values, and traditions.

Change is required to acquire new skills and become an expert in your field. You must take action to create change and adapt and grow when necessary while maintaining the things that bring us a sense of comfort and meaning. By doing so, you can make progress while feeling grounded and connected to what is essential to you. *Find a balance between change and stability to navigate life's challenges.*

Action and the Pace of Change

The pace of change is much faster today than in the past, and the nature of change has also changed. The current changes are more complex and unpredictable and require different strategies to cope with them.

The military and policy circles coined the term V-U-C-A. **VUCA** *stands for* **volatility, uncertainty, complexity, and ambiguity.** Volatility refers to the unexpected and unstable challenges that arise with unknown durations. Uncertainty refers to the lack of predictability and the unknown outcomes of events. Complexity is when many interconnected variables make events hard to understand and manage. Ambiguity is when events lack clarity and have multiple interpretations, making it hard to know what to do.

VUCA: To deal with volatility, prepare for unexpected challenges with flexible backup plans. For uncertainty, focus on building resilience by diversifying resources and investing in adaptable systems. To handle complexity, analyze data, and work with experts to understand the interconnected variables and their impact. When facing ambiguity, communicate clearly, seek feedback, and stay open-minded to different interpretations.

VUCA can apply to individuals in their daily lives, employees in their careers, and solo entrepreneurs in several ways.

Life can be full of VUCA challenges like unexpected events, uncertain outcomes, complex decisions, and ambiguous situations. Develop a open mind, embrace change, learn from failures, and adapt to new conditions. Build a support network to provide resources, advice, and encouragement to help cope with VUCA challenges.

VUCA challenges in a career can be caused by changing job requirements, uncertain job security, complex work tasks, and ambiguous performance expectations. Employees can seek feedback, continuously learn, and build supportive relationships with coworkers and mentors. They can also be proactive in their career development by seeking new experiences and expanding their skill set.

Entrepreneurs who work independently may face VUCA challenges such as unpredictable market conditions, complex business decisions, unexpected competition, and unclear customer needs. To tackle these challenges, they can keep themselves up-to-date on market trends, use data analysis to make informed decisions, be flexible to changes in customer needs, and build connections with other entrepreneurs and mentors for guidance and support.

To overcome challenges and succeed in their personal and professional lives, individuals, employees, and entrepreneurs can use the principles of VUCA. They can thrive in a rapidly changing world by developing resilience, engaging learning opportunities, and building solid relationships.

Action in Work & Productivity

"Inspiration exists, but it has to find you working." ~Pablo Picasso

To be successful, find work that you enjoy and is worthy of your time and talent. Take the initiative, constantly improve, prioritize quality, and persist. Aim for meaningful and productive work, set high standards, and strive for continual growth.

To achieve greatness, two essential elements are to set high standards and execute persistently. High standards is to strive for excellence and hold yourself accountable. Persistent execution means consistent effort, discipline, and overcoming setbacks.

Greatness is not accidental. Greatness is a deliberate and sustained effort to maintain high standards and execute persistently.

High standards can increase motivation, build self-confidence and create a sense of progress.

To achieve great things and leave a lasting legacy, it's important to have a clear vision in your enhavim, commit to excellence, and work hard even in the face of adversity.

Setting high standards is an essential part of personal and professional development. One of the key benefits of setting high standards is that it increases motivation and drive. Having clarity with a set of criteria you want to achieve can energize and inspire you. This motivation can help you stay focused and committed despite obstacles and setbacks. Setting high standards can also lead to greater self-confidence and self-esteem. When you consistently meet or exceed your expectations build trust and belief in yourself, it carries over into other areas of your life.

Setting high standards does not mean setting unrealistic or unachievable goals. They should be "stretchingly" realistic goals. Setting realistic yet challenging standards can give you a sense of momentum toward your goals, leading to fulfillment and achievement. This involves challenging yourself to aim for excellence while being mindful of your capabilities and limitations.

Actions and Your Type

Did you know that your type of action-taking may be affected by how you see the world: idealist, cynic, or realist?

Actions for an idealist is someone who holds an optimistic view of the world and believes in the power of long-term goals and ideals. They may be willing to sacrifice short-term gains or pleasures to pursue a greater good, such as social justice or world peace.

On the other hand, cynics tend to be skeptical or distrustful of other people's motivations and the possibility of long-term change. They may view short-term gains as the only measure of success and be resigned to the idea that the world is inherently flawed or corrupt.

Realists understand that short-term actions can have long-term consequences. They recognize the importance of setting and achieving short-term goals while keeping the long-term in mind. They are pragmatic problem solvers who strive to balance short-term and long-term considerations.

Most individuals tend towards laziness or complacency. People who strive for greatness are distinguished not only by their innate intelligence or abilities but also by certain characteristics. These characteristics include curiosity, energy, the drive to use their full potential, and a willingness to push themselves to their limits. You may need to be made aware of your full potential, and it often takes some incentive or motivation to bring out your best qualities. This could be in the form of challenges, opportunities, or simply a deep desire to achieve a particular goal.

Human beings have been endowed with a vast array of talents and abilities by a higher power ("God"), but you may not fully realize or appreciate these gifts. It is up to you to tap into this potential. By recognizing your potential and striving to make the most of it, you can achieve greatness and positively impact the world around you. The fruition of this potential takes place through your actions.

Action and Adaptability

When do you know when to change your actions? It may be necessary to give up the life you have planned to set into the life that is waiting for you. Deciding to change course can be tough because it means giving up goals or expectations you've been working towards for a long time. It's important to recognize that your current path may not be the best fit for you. Other opportunities or paths may lead to greater happiness and fulfillment.

By letting go of the life you have planned, you create space for new experiences and opportunities to come into your life. This can be a time of significant growth and learning as you explore new paths and discover unique aspects of yourself. It requires an open mind and a willingness to embrace uncertainty and change, but the rewards can be tremendous.

It's also important to recognize that giving up the life you have planned does not mean abandoning your beliefs or aspirations. Instead, it means being open to new possibilities and allowing yourself to be guided by your intuition and inner wisdom. This can involve taking risks, stepping outside of your comfort zone, and being willing to learn from both successes and failures.

Of course, the decision to give up the life you have planned is profoundly personal, and it requires courage and self-awareness. Be open to new experiences and opportunities that may lead to a more fulfilling and purposeful life aligned with your true passions. This may be your most important decision and action.

Time and Prioritizing Actions:

"Time is more valuable than money. You can get more money, but you cannot get more time." ~Jim Rohn

We all know we must focus on critical, non-urgent tasks rather than reacting to urgent but less important demands.

Our perception of time is influenced by language, memory, and culture. It is closely linked to our capacity to envision and act upon future events (act being the operative word).

Carlo Rovelli's book "The Order of Time" examines the concept of time and how humans perceive and construct it. Rovelli suggests that humans create order by breaking time into units and that time is a cultural and cognitive construct. He explores how language, memory, and culture affect our perception of time and how time is linked to our ability to imagine and act on future events.

How we organize time using lunar months, solar years, or other units of time reflects the values and priorities of our society. We humans use units of time (day, week, month) to organize our lives and create a sense of rhythm and structure in the world around us.

There is a relationship between time and memory, and our use of units of time is closely tied to our ability to remember the past and imagine the future. By organizing our lives into units of time we create a framework for remembering events, developing habits, and planning future activities.

We use time to plan and then act.

We also act spontaneously, and also this happens in time.

Time and action are intimately entwined.

Time is an aspect of our existence and influences nearly every part of our lives, including our actions. Without time, there would be no past, present, or future, and the concept of action would cease.

The concept of time is fundamental to our understanding of the world. Although time itself is fixed and does not change, your decisions and subsequent actions happen during a specific period. It is your action that affects your life and the world. You have the power to choose how you use your time daily. Making deliberate choices on how you engage your time allows you to make valuable contributions towards your goals and the world around you.

What's most important is that you value the impact your actions have on your life and the world around you. Taking actions that align with your priorities and goals can make a positive impact and create a meaningful life. It is important to be intentional about how you spend your time and to prioritize activities that align with your values and goals. For example, if your goal is to learn a new skill, you may need to take action daily to practice and study. If you prioritize sharing time with loved ones, you may need to factor social activities and quality time into your schedule.

It's also important to recognize that the impact of your actions can extend beyond your immediate circumstances. The choices you make and the actions you take can have a ripple effect that impacts others and the world around you. By being mindful of your actions and their impact, you can make a positive difference in the lives of others and contribute to a better world.

One of the keys to valuing what you do with your time is to have a clear sense of purpose and direction. When you clearly understand your goals and what you want to achieve, you can make more intentional choices about how you act.

Establishing healthy habits and routines can help you make the most of your personal life. Set a regular sleep schedule, prioritize exercise and healthy eating, and set aside time each day for meditation or reflection. This helps you can streamline your daily activities and support your goals and priorities.

Timing is essential in many areas of life, such as business, sports, and relationships. A well-timed action can make all the difference in achieving a goal or accomplishing a task. Time is often a crucial factor in determining the success or failure of our actions.

To achieve your goals, prioritize one main thing that is more important than anything else. Guard your time so that it is utilized wisely by focusing on your one yearning. By concentrating on your one yearning, success can be achieved.

Our present choices can significantly impact our future. Managing our time effectively is crucial to each desired outcome. Time management (better phrased as 'managing your actions') and planning are essential skills. This enables us to make the most available time to achieve our goals and fulfill our responsibilities.

Having a plan is essential to achieve our goals in life, just like planning a trip. You may get in a car for a joyride, but would you go to the airport and get on any plane without knowing the destination? It may fun to be spontaneous but it would be best if you had a specific plan. IT's important to keep planning simple and avoid unnecessary complications. Occam's razor suggests that if there are two solutions to a problem, choose the simpler one. A convoluted plan can be a result of fear of failure or success. A complex plan can deceive us into thinking we're making progress when we're going around in circles.

Knowing how time and action are intertwined can help us utilize our time better and reach the greatness we yearn for.

Actions can happen at any time, depending on the specific context and purpose of the action, with three parts: 1. start, 2. middle, 3. end. The beginning, progress, and finish of action can occur quickly or slowly, depending on the course of the activity.

SHORT-TERM ACTIONS: These can happen whenever you need them, depending on the type and time required for completion. Short-term actions are typically finished in a short period, like a few hours or days, while long-term efforts can take weeks, months, or even years. To ensure you're making progress, divide the activities into smaller tasks and assign a timeline to each. Then, add these tasks to your schedule to guarantee they're completed within the specified timeline.

Here are examples of short-term personal *actions:*

Short-term personal actions include committing to reading a book each week, setting aside time for exercise each day (maybe 75 Hard?), or starting a budgeting regimen. Small, achievable steps can form the foundation for a more prosperous future. This could involve improving physical, mental, and emotional health and learning new skills and knowledge that could lead to greater career opportunities.

Here are examples of short-term professional *actions:*

What are the quick wins you can take in your professional career? Professional activities could involve setting up a weekly meeting with a mentor, creating a list of goals and action items to complete each day, or researching a potential new job opportunity. Short-term professional activities are focused, measurable, and directly contribute to achieving long-term career goals. Show that you're willing to go the extra mile is a great way to demonstrate your value to employers and colleagues.

A sales professional may take short-term actions such as conducting market research, prospecting for potential clients, and creating sales presentations. An engineer may focus on attending industry events, updating their technical skills, and collaborating with colleagues to solve complex problems. A teacher may take actions such as designing lesson plans, providing individual feedback to students, and attending professional development workshops.

Taking proactive steps to stay ahead of the curve is critical. A marketer could focus on learning the latest marketing trends, experimenting with different strategies, and creating content that resonates with their target audience. A doctor could research medical advancements, hone their interpersonal skills, and collaborate with other medical professionals to provide the best care for their patients. A lawyer could attend relevant seminars, network with colleagues, and stay informed on the latest legal developments. Taking the initiative to stay informed and on top of your field can be the difference between success and failure.

Writing is a great way to take action for your short and long-term actions. No matter what you're working towards, committing to writing something daily can help you progress. Even if it's just a few sentences, the act of writing can help you take action and stay motivated. Plus, it's a great way to practice and hone your writing skills to express yourself. Start writing today!

LONG-TERM ACTIONS: These are actions that require a significant amount of time and effort to complete, such as pursuing a degree, training for a marathon, or starting a business. Break these goals into smaller, more manageable tasks and assign a timeline for each task. Create a plan with deadlines and schedule these tasks into your calendar to ensure consistent progress toward completing the action within the desired timeframe. It's also essential to assess your progress and adjust your plan to stay on track and achieve your long-term goals.

Here are examples of long-term personal *actions:*

Achieving marathons or triathlons, slimming down, bulking up, taking on a new exercise program, or creating a healthy diet are several ways to reach your fitness goals.

Investing time into a lasting relationship, deepening ties with family and friends, meeting new people, or improving communication are ways to build relationship connections.

Developing a regular meditation practice, taking a deeper dive into your faith, cultivating gratitude, or committing to a spiritual or religious practice are ways to explore your spirituality.

Renovating, constructing, landscaping, or making energy-efficient changes to your home are ways to upgrade your living space.

Learning a new language, getting a higher certification, honing a new skill or hobby, and volunteering are ways to develop yourself.

Investing for the future, getting out of debt, setting up a savings plan, or getting extra schooling are ways to plan for your financial future.

Another massive long-term action is to start a business or side hustle. This may take time and effort, but it can ultimately pay off. You could be working for yourself and making money from something you are passionate about.

Here are examples of long-term professional *actions:*

Taking long-term professional action means going the extra mile for success. It could mean honing a new skill, creating a portfolio to showcase your abilities, or networking with industry professionals to gain insight into the field. It could also mean taking on a new challenge, such as a new job or project, to expand your experience. Take the initiative to invest in yourself, and a great way to set yourself up for greatness.

Pursuing a medical degree, getting a specialty certification, doing a residency or fellowship program, inventing a new treatment or therapy, or researching clinical studies are all long-term professional actions in the healthcare industry.

You can start a new business, create a product or service, expand into a fresh market, develop a long-term marketing or branding approach to a product or business.

For the education sector, you could obtain an MBA or Ph.D., craft a new curriculum or teaching method, obtain an administrative role, lead a major school or district project, or devise and implement a long-term fundraising or development plan.

In technology, you could make a new software or hardware product, get an advanced computer science or engineering degree, manage a major development project or team, develop and execute a long-term technology approach, or do cutting-edge research in a given field.

You could get a law degree specializing in a particular development area with a new legal theory or approach, establish a new law practice or firm, or direct a significant legal case or initiative.

When it comes to financing, you could pursue an advanced degree in finance or accounting, focus on a particular area of finance such as investment banking or financial planning, devise a long-term investment strategy, or make a significant financial effort or project.

Creative industries involve developing a new creative work or project such as a book, film, or music album, creating a solid portfolio or body of work, forming a long-term creative vision or approach, or doing advanced training or education in a specialized area of the creative arts.

HABITS: Habits are actions that can be short-term or long-term and may occur at any time during the day or week, depending on the specific habit and individual's schedule. Identify which habits you want to develop or maintain, and schedule them into your calendar at a particular time each day or week. For example, if you're going to exercise every morning, schedule it into your calendar as a recurring activity.

Here are examples of personal habits:

Short-term personal habits include taking breaks, setting goals, and tracking progress. Short-term habits can consist of snacking, TV watching-binging, and a slew of other less beneficial habits worth noting over a week.

Taking care of yourself can also help you avoid burnout and maintain a positive outlook. Taking charge of your health is also an essential step to achieving success. Eating a balanced diet, exercising regularly, and getting enough sleep can help you stay mentally and physically sharp to focus on your goals.

Making and sticking to a plan can help you stay on track with your goals. Setting daily, weekly, and monthly goals can help you stay motivated and measure your progress. It's also important to have self-reflection time to assess your progress. This can help you make adjustments and keep you focused on your goals.

Here are examples of long-term personal *habits:*

Long-term personal habits include exercising regularly, eating a balanced diet, and getting enough sleep. Have a daily routine that includes activities that help you to relax and de-stress.

Physical: Rejuvenation can involve stretching, yoga, or a massage to help recharge the body. Resting can include sleeping, napping, or simply lying down to give the body time to recover.

Mental: Schedule short breaks throughout the day for processing and reflection. Jotting down nagging or intrusive thoughts can also help to clear the mind and allow for rest. It can be helpful to read a book or listen to a podcast that interests you, engage in a stimulating conversation with someone, learn a new skill, or take a class in a subject that fascinates you.

Emotional: It can be beneficial to take a break from people-pleasing and respond to requests authentically with your true feelings and capacity. Setting meaningful boundaries with others, balancing work and personal time, and releasing pent-up emotions can help provide emotional rest.

Spiritual: Connect to a higher power through meditation, prayer, or community involvement. Spending time outdoors or in the presence of beauty can also help to provide spiritual rest and renewal.

Creative: Posting art that you love in your workspace can also inspire creativity. Making something with your hands, such as cooking, doing a puzzle, drawing, or putting together furniture, can also help to recharge creativity.

Social: Enjoy more time with people that revive you and less time with people that exhaust you. Turning down invites that don't appeal to you can also help to provide social rest. Initiating or saying yes to opportunities to do activities you genuinely enjoy doing with others can also help to recharge socially.

Environmental: Spend time in nature, surround yourself with plants, fresh air, and natural light, declutter and organize your living space, or invest in a quality air purifier or water filter.

Sensory: To recharge the senses, it can be helpful to periodically close your eyes and unplug from electronics, light, noise, and other stimuli. Limiting your screen time and being mindful of when you're using technology and when you're not can also help you to stay connected with the present moment. Lying down for 20 minutes and doing absolutely nothing can also help to provide sensory rest.

Here are examples of professional *habits:*

Professional habits include showing up to work on time, working efficiently, and staying organized.

Staying current on industry news, trends, and technology is also essential. Developing a network of colleagues and staying connected with them can also be beneficial. Networking can help you remain in the know and gain insight from professionals in your field. Taking the time to network can open up doors to potential opportunities and collaborations. Furthermore, developing a growth mindset and striving for continuous improvement can help you become more successful in your career. This can include learning new skills and actively pursuing knowledge to stay ahead of the competition.

Maintaining a positive attitude, remaining proactive, and staying focused on your objectives is essential. Adapting to changes quickly and handling unexpected due tasks are also necessary for success in the workplace. Moreover, developing a solid work ethic and having a commitment to excellence will help you stand out and make a lasting impression. With the proper habits, you can pave the way to success.

Here are examples of long-term professional *habits:*

Professional habits should also include developing skills to help you stay ahead of the competition and progress in your career. This could mean learning new technologies, developing communication skills, and staying updated with industry news.

Professional habits include attending industry events, networking with people in your field, and reading industry news.

Hone your problem-solving skills and your ability to work with a team. Working in a collaborative environment and understanding dynamics can incredibly benefit your career. Developing a solid work ethic and time management skills is also essential. Stay organized and ensure a sound system for tracking your progress and goals. Good habits can help you stay ahead and reach your goals.

JOB-ENTREPRENEUR-BUSINESS-LIVELIHOOD: Actions related to work or business may happen during regular business hours, or outside of typical work hours, depending on the specific job or industry. Entrepreneurs may work irregular hours as they build and grow their businesses, while those with traditional jobs may work regular 9-to-5 hours. Schedule your work hours and any additional time needed for meetings, emails, or projects. If you're an entrepreneur or business owner, factor in time for planning, networking, and marketing.

Here are examples of intelligent actions you can take related to your job, your livelihood, being an entrepreneur, and running your business:

Actions related to your job, livelihood, and business can help you reach your full potential. For instance, if you're an entrepreneur, you can take steps to ensure streamlined processes, automate tasks, and create systems that allow you to do more with less.

If you're looking to make a career change, it's essential to research your potential field and create a plan for how you'll transition. This could mean creating a list of skills you need to acquire, reaching out to people in the industry, and attending conferences and workshops to learn more. If you're already employed, look for ways to increase your value to your employer, such as taking on new responsibilities or seeking new growth opportunities.

You can also take action related to your finances. Whether taking a course on personal finance or investing in stocks, there are plenty of ways to grow your wealth. You can even start a side business to bring in extra income.

No matter your current situation, taking action can help you achieve success. Take the time to network and build relationships with those who can help you further your goals.

TALENT-SKILL: Developing and practicing talent or skill can happen anytime but often requires dedicated time and effort. Many practice their skills outside 'school' hours, such as evenings or weekends. Determine the best time of day or week to practice your talent or skill, and schedule it into your calendar as a recurring activity. You could also set a specific goal, such as learning a new song or completing a project, and set a deadline for yourself to keep you motivated. Dedicating yourself to regular practice and setting realistic goals can help you reach your full potential and satisfy you when you are done.

Here are examples of Talent-Skill development actions:

Learning an Instrument: Improve your skills, experiment with different songs and styles, and discover new techniques and music theory.

Put Pen to Paper: Create a writing habit - whether writing for a set period on your work or completing a writing project.

Mastering a Language: Invest in yourself and commit to studying vocab, grammar, and conversation - whether through classes, language exchanges, or self-teaching.

Bring Art to Life: Make time for practice and exploration, take art classes or workshops, and share your creations with others for feedback.

Learn to Code: Schedule some coding sessions to familiarize yourself with new languages, build projects and apps, and try coding challenges or competitions.

Cook Your Way to Success: Create a regular cooking regimen, try new recipes and techniques, practice the basics, and specialize in something unique.

Get Comfortable with Public Speaking: Set aside time to practice your public speaking abilities, prepare and deliver speeches, join speaking groups or competitions, and get feedback on your communication and presentation skills.

LEARNING: Learning can happen at any time, but it is typically a long-term process that involves ongoing efforts to acquire new knowledge, skills, and competencies. Learning can occur informally in formal settings such as schools or universities through self-directed study or experiences. Identify specific times during the day or week when you can dedicate time to learning, whether attending a class, studying online, or reading a book. Schedule these times into your calendar and treat them as non-negotiable commitments.

William James, an American philosopher and psychologist, said, *"The great aim of education is not knowledge but action."*

Here are examples of learning actions:

This could range from brushing up on existing skills to learning an entirely new skill or language.

It's essential to stay informed. Read (or listen to) books, articles, blogs, and videos related to your industry, and attend seminars and networking events to keep current on the latest trends. This will help you stay ahead of the curve and be competitive in your field.

Consider taking classes to increase your knowledge and hone your skills.

Enrolling in classes is a great way to stay ahead of the game and competitive. You can learn new skills and broaden your existing knowledge base. Take online courses to further your education. Utilizing online resources such as online tutorials and webinars are great ways to stay informed in your industry.

Use social media platforms to stay connected and get the latest updates. Participate in online communities and forums to network and get feedback from other professionals in your field. Personally, I enjoy attending conferences or seminars to keep up with the ever-evolving trends, reconnect with colleagues, and stay ahead of the competition.

HOBBIES-ART-TRAVEL-RECREATION: These actions are typically pursued outside of work or school hours and may occur at any time, depending on personal preferences and schedules. Please plan for any trips or events related to these activities, and schedule them into your calendar well in advance. For ongoing hobbies or artistic pursuits, schedule regular time for these activities, such as a weekly painting class or monthly book club meeting.

Engage in activities that bring you joy and relaxation, such as reading a book, walking, or spending time with friends. Giving yourself the time and space to regroup and refocus can be invaluable on your journey to success. Why not try something new?

Here are examples of Hobbies-Art-Travel-Recreation actions:

Hiking: If you want to get outdoors and explore, plan regular hikes and other outdoor activities, such as day trips or weekend camping trips, and save them on your calendar in advance.

Photography: Dedicate a few hours each week to practice or plan a photo shoot at a specific location. Keep track of your progress with a log or app.

Reading: Join a book club or block off time for regular reading (or listening) on a regular schedule. Perhaps use a log or app to track your progress.

Painting: Take an art class, or make room in your schedule for painting sessions, either weekly or daily.

Travel: Researching and booking flights, accommodations, and visas can be time-consuming, so plan and schedule trips and travel experiences ahead.

Yoga-Meditation: Schedule some time for yoga or meditation, whether a daily routine or a weekly class.

Cooking: Plan for cooking experiences such as trying new recipes, hosting dinner parties, or taking classes or workshops. Make sure you set aside enough time for it.

LEGACY-CHARITY-CAUSES: People may choose to engage in actions related to legacy, charity, or causes at any time based on their unique objectives and preferences. For instance, one may commit a substantial amount of time and resources to these areas, while another may participate sporadically. To contribute to these causes, determine which charities or causes matter to you and set aside time in your schedule for volunteer work or fundraising. You may also set clear goals for your legacy, such as authoring a book or establishing a scholarship fund, and block out time in your calendar to work on those endeavors. Be legacy worthy.

Here are examples of Legacy-Charity-Causes actions:

Volunteer: Regularly offer your time to an organization or cause you to care about.

Fundraising: Use creative methods to raise money for charity or causes you support.

Donate: Prioritize donations and set up recurring contributions to causes that matter to you.

Advocate: Speak out for issues and causes you to believe in by attending rallies or writing to legislators.

Legacy Planning: Create a plan for leaving a lasting legacy through actions like establishing trust or creating a will.

Mentor: Volunteer your time to mentor others in your field or community.

Community Service: Identify areas of need and regularly volunteer in your community.

Taking action toward meaningful activities can help you find purpose, direction, and fulfillment, leading to success, expertise, and greatness. Taking action is the outward expression of the 5 core values. The YEARN Advantage can help you progress towards your goals and feel energized by the results. Commit to excellence and high standards to make a positive impact. This theme repeats daily.

"Don't miss out on opportunities. Act now!"

Opportunities come and go quickly, so it's essential to be aware of them and take action as soon as possible. This applies to all aspects of life, including personal and professional endeavors. To spot opportunities, keep an open mind, evaluate risks, stay informed, and network. Take action when you identify an opportunity by starting projects, handling failure constructively, and having a bias for action.

Accountability is also important for achieving greatness, so define your goals, set actionable targets, keep your motivation in mind, and track your progress. Seize every opportunity given to you because once they expire, they may not come around again.

REVIEW Question for 'ACT'

• What do you want to DO?

Related to "YOU" Question: Why do you want to do it?

R - What does Money have to do with it?

"Money is only a tool. It will take you wherever you wish but will not replace you as the driver."
~Ayn Rand

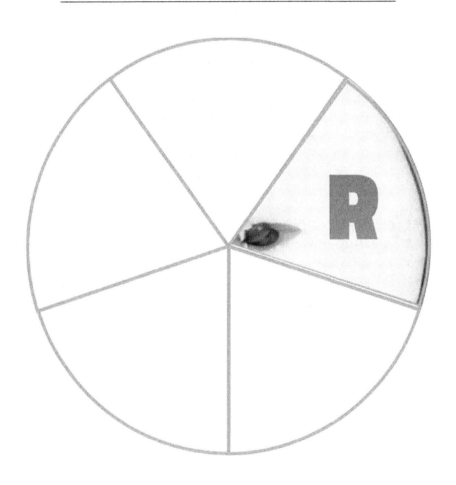

RESOURCES
IS CORE VALUE #4

"R amp up your resources; it's a great strategy with lasting rewards!"

How do your RESOURCE AVAILABILITY and FINANCIAL CHOICES reflect your priorities and aspirations?

The "Resources" core value of the YEARN Advantage emphasizes identifying and acquiring the tangible and intangible resources necessary for achieving our goals. To plan and use your time and resources well, identify what you need to succeed. This might include physical things like tools, materials, or money, and less concrete things like knowledge, skills, and people to support you. By knowing and addressing what you need, you can set yourself up for success and make the most of your resources.

Questions for "RESOURCES"

- **What do you need to do it?**
- **What tangible resources do I need to achieve this goal, such as money or equipment?**
- **What intangible resources do I need, such as knowledge or skills?**
- **What challenges or obstacles may I face, and what resources will I need to overcome them?**

Access to resources is fundamental to realizing your dreams and leading a fulfilling life. These resources can help you pursue your ambitions, whether related to career development, self-growth, or positive influence.

Financial resources, in particular, give you a sense of security and stability. Knowing that you possess the resources to meet your present necessities and goals can alleviate your worries and minimize stress. This can free up your mental and emotional power to concentrate on other areas of your life and pursue your dreams.

Resources that you can utilize go beyond financial resources. Tools, education, talents, and connections are all resources that can aid in achieving your objectives. Relationships with other people can give you access to their assets and financial resources.

Learning how to use your resources skillfully and strategically is crucial. This means understanding your available resources and how to use them to your advantage. To achieve your goals, you need to have a certain level of financial literacy and an understanding of your strengths and weaknesses. This may require you to learn new skills or obtain resources.

At the same time, it's important to remember that resources do not guarantee success. It's up to you to put in the effort, take risks, and make the most of the chances that come your way. Keep your attitude positive attitude while utilizing the available resources.

Resources come in different forms including financial assets, educational opportunities, tools, personal skills, and connections. Maximizing these resources can help you achieve your goals. Financial resources help you can invest in your education, start a business, or travel the world.

Education can provide the necessary knowledge and skills to pursue your interests and career path. Tools and equipment can increase efficiency and effectiveness, especially when starting a business. Personal talents can set you apart in your field. Networking can create new opportunities.

> *"Still, I suppose we must work with the tools we have."* ~*Superior Goyle*
> The Blade Itself by Joe Abercrombie

Why do people look outside themselves and their existing resources to succeed? Work to maximize your existing assets and resources to get where you want to go. Use the tools you have at your disposal.

Financial resources are important, but knowledge and skills are also valuable to live a purposeful life. Pursuing education and training to obtain a degree or certification, learning a new language, or developing new skills can open up new opportunities.

Investing in education is a valuable way to use your resources to pursue your goals. Education can take different forms, such as formal schooling, online courses, or self-directed learning. Gaining relevant knowledge and skills in your desired field can increase your value to potential employers and improve your chances of success.

Success comes from developing a unique set of skills that contribute value to society. This requires patience, focus, and persistence. Wealth can be attained by creating something people want rather than chasing money. Building something of value that people will pay for can lead to financial gain.

Resources give us the power and control to direct our lives and pursue our dreams. However, more than simply having access to these resources is required. We must also learn to use them effectively and strategically to create lasting change and achieve our goals. Combining financial resources with knowledge and skills can create a strong foundation for a meaningful and satisfying life.

Learning new things can help us discover more about ourselves and our capabilities. We can better understand our potential and strengths when we challenge ourselves. Step out of the comfort zone and pursue education. Training can lead to new relationships and connections when networking with others with similar goals.

Learning new skills and gaining knowledge can be a rewarding experience in itself. Networking opportunities and connections with other learners can lead to potential collaborations. Networking is the next value of the YEARN Advantage.

Having the resources to pursue your passions is essential, as it helps you manifest your dreams and can lead to recognition and status. Resources are not just limited to finances. They can also include personal connections, access to assets and information, or having the right attitude.

The right attitude can be an excellent resource for achieving success. An open and positive mindset allows for creativity and increases the chances of finding new opportunities. Use resources such as technology or social networks to proactively seek opportunities. Build relationships with like-minded individuals to gain new insights to stay on top of trends with a competitive edge.

To make the most of your resources, you must understand what you have and how to use them effectively. This involves not only identifying your resources, but also assessing your strengths and weaknesses. With this knowledge, you can create a plan with concrete steps for utilizing your resources most effectively.

Due to the limited resources, consider eliminating what is not required. For example, pruning a fruit tree directs growth to the new branches and fruit. Similarly, in our own lives, we can prune away unnecessary habits, possessions, and activities that drain our energy. This allows for better utilization of the existing resources.

Using the resources and tools at your disposal can empower you and give you a sense of purpose. You don't have to let yourself be restricted by external limitations; instead, craft your future with self-belief, courage, and enthusiasm.

We can approach our lives with more confidence and positivity when we have ample resources, whether they are financial, temporal, or otherwise. This confidence comes from knowing that we have the necessary means to handle challenges that may come our way. It's not about having enough resources to get by; it's about having a surplus that allows us to take risks and invest in our future.

One key benefit of adequate resources is that it reduces stress levels. Worrying about making ends meet or struggling to find the time to get everything done can take a toll on our mental and emotional state. When we have enough resources to cover our basic needs and pursue our goals, we can focus our attention and energy on what truly matters.

Money, Power, & Reputation Resources

Money, power, and reputation are all highly desirable resources that can be borrowed, negotiated, and leveraged to achieve objectives. These resources can be classified as either tangible or intangible.

"Are you resourced?" is a phrase commonly used in British English. It is an inquiry to see if someone or something has the essential resources required to operate efficiently. The term "resourced" may encompass a range of resources for a particular task or project. The question asks whether the person or entity has all the tools they need to succeed. For instance, if someone asks, "Are you resourced for this project?" they are being asked if they have adequate

resources, including time, money, equipment, materials, personnel, or other necessary resources to successfully complete the project.

Money Resource

Money can be used to attain various goals, such as starting a business, buying a home, or investing in education.

When leveraging money, here are some things to consider:

- Money can be tangible such as physical currency, or intangible, such as digital currency used in online banking or digital payment systems.

- To manage money effectively, it is important to have financial literacy and discipline to ensure it is used wisely and for its intended purpose.

- Protect digital money from theft or fraud by using strong passwords, avoiding phishing scams, and using trusted payment systems.

- When borrowing money, it's important to understand the terms of the agreement and manage the repayment effectively to avoid future financial difficulties.

- Establishing a budget can help you keep track of your spending and ensure you are not overspending or going into debt.

- Investing can be a way to grow your wealth over time. It's essential to understand the risks and potential returns before investing.

- Creating an emergency fund can provide a safety net in case of unexpected expenses or loss of income.

- Consider seeking the advice of a financial professional to help you make informed decisions about your money.

Power-Influence Resource

Power can be used to achieve objectives by influencing decision-making and accessing resources. It can take different forms, including coercive, reward, expert, and legitimate authority. Coercive power uses punishment for noncompliance, while reward power uses incentives for compliance. Expert power is based on specialized knowledge, and legitimate power comes from formal positions or titles that grant authority over others.

When leveraging power, here are some things to consider:

- Power is an intangible resource that can achieve various objectives, such as influencing decision-making or gaining access to resources.

- To use power effectively, it is important to understand the context and relationships between individuals and groups.

- Negotiating power and forming alliances with others with similar goals or interests can help you achieve your objectives.

- Using power responsibly and ethically is crucial to maintaining trust and credibility.

- When faced with a power struggle, staying calm and focused on your goals while remaining respectful and professional towards others is important.

- Building a network of relationships and establishing a positive reputation can help you leverage your power effectively.

- Consider seeking the advice of a mentor or coach to help you navigate complex power dynamics in your personal or professional life.

Reputation Resource

Here are some things to consider when managing and protecting your reputation:

- Reputation is an intangible resource built through consistent effort and ethical behavior over time. It can enhance your credibility and open doors to new opportunities.

- Respect and recognition are key components of reputation, and they are earned through your actions and interactions with others.

- A positive reputation can be leveraged to attain various goals, such as gaining new clients or advancing your career.

- Maintaining a positive reputation requires ongoing engagement with others, delivering on promises and commitments, and treating others with respect and dignity.

- Factors outside your control, such as public perception or media coverage, can also affect your reputation.

- Actively managing and protecting your reputation is crucial and can involve monitoring your online presence, responding to negative feedback or reviews professionally, and being transparent and honest in your interactions with others.

- Developing strong communication skills, including listening actively and providing clear and concise messages, can help you build a positive reputation.

- Building a network of relationships and establishing a positive personal brand can also help you effectively manage and protect your reputation.

Power and reputation combined become a "referent" resource for being admired, respected, or liked by others. Celebrities or popular leaders may have referent power over their followers.

Referent power is a type of power that is based on personal characteristics that make a person attractive or likable to others. These characteristics may include charisma, trustworthiness, expertise, and interpersonal skills. When people admire or respect someone, they may be more likely to follow their lead or comply with their requests.

Famous people or leaders can have referent power by having a large following that admires them. Athletes or musicians may influence their fans with their accomplishments or personality. Political leaders can have referent power if they are viewed as honest, competent, and caring.

Referent power allows people to influence others without coercion or rewards. People with referent power can inspire others to adopt their values or beliefs and motivate them to act towards a common goal. Referent power is considered more authentic and enduring compared to other types of power. Referent power is built on a personal relationship between the leader and their followers.

An online influencer has built a significant resource of followers on social media platforms, such as Instagram, YouTube, or TikTok. Influencers often specialize in a particular niche or interest area. This could be fashion, beauty, fitness, travel, or food. Influencers leverage their personal brand to promote related products or services. They can influence the purchasing decisions of their followers with their recommendations.

Online influencers with referent power may have a strong connection with their followers. Their followers look up to them as role models or experts in their niche. These influencers can inspire their audience to adopt their values or beliefs and motivate them to take action. Influencers must maintain transparency with followers.

If the person wielding their referent resource does not have the best interests of their followers in mind, they may manipulate their followers or exploit their trust. Some leaders may use their charisma or popularity to take advantage of their followers. Misusing referent power can lead to a loss of trust and damage their brand. It is essential to use referent resources responsibly and ethically.

A referent resource is a combination of personal qualities such as reputation, respect, and likability that one can use to influence others. To use this resource effectively, it's important to have additional skills such as financial literacy, strategic thinking, marketing, and solid interpersonal skills.

Are You Resourceful?

When someone asks if you are resourceful enough to find a solution, they generally ask whether you have the skills and talent to find a solution. The question asks whether you can identify and utilize the resources necessary to solve the problem at hand.

To solve problems effectively, one requires skills, knowledge, and creativity, regardless of the resources available. Resources can be tangible, such as tools, equipment, and money, or intangible, such as problem-solving skills and critical thinking ability. Being resourceful entails finding a way to attain the desired result using available resources, acquiring or developing additional resources by collaborating with others, and adapting to unexpected challenges. Being resourceful requires thought and action.

Entrepreneurs and Resources

If you want to start a new business or venture, you need resources. Getting funding is essential to bring your ideas to fruition. Here are various options, traditional and more modern:

Bootstrapping: This is a self-funding approach where entrepreneurs use their own resources to start the business. This can include personal savings, credit cards, or borrowing money from friends and family.

Grants: Some organizations, including government agencies, private foundations, and non-profit organizations, offer grants to entrepreneurs. These grants can fund research and development, marketing, and other business-related expenses. Grants do not require repayment but are often highly competitive.

Crowdfunding is a relatively new way to fund a new business, where many individuals contribute small amounts of money to a project or venture. This can be done through online platforms like Kickstarter or Indiegogo, which allow entrepreneurs to create a profile and pitch their idea to a broad audience. If the project is successful, the entrepreneur receives the funds pledged by the contributors.

Angel investors: Angel investors fund startups or small businesses in exchange for equity. They are typically wealthy individuals interested in supporting new ventures and can provide mentorship and networking opportunities.

Bank loans: A bank loan is a traditional way to fund a business. Entrepreneurs can apply for a loan, which they must pay with interest over time. The loan and interest rates will depend on various factors, such as the business plan, credit history, and collateral.

Venture capital is a form of financing where investors provide funds to a startup or a business in exchange for an equity stake. Venture capital firms typically invest in businesses that have high growth potential but are also high-risk ventures. In exchange for the investment, the venture capitalist will have a say in the company's decisions and share in its profits.

Funding a new business or venture is a challenging endeavor with many options. From traditional bank loans to modern approaches such as crowdfunding and venture capital, entrepreneurs must weigh the pros and cons of each and decide which is best for their goals.

To make the most of the resources available, one must be able to sell their ideas to others. This requires persuading and influencing others to exchange their resources for what you offer. More than 40 percent of our work time is spent on non-sales selling, like pitching ideas and convincing funders to support projects. The key to success is creating conditions that demonstrate the potential benefits of parting with valuable resources, such as investing in a venture that will yield future growth.

Selling ideas requires more than problem-solving. It involves understanding decision-makers biases and preferences, interpreting data, and considering various options. This helps investors better see the potential benefit of investing their resources.

Benefit of Resources

Having adequate resources provides a sense of stability that can be comforting and motivating. When we know that we have enough money or time to accomplish what we need, we are more likely to stay on track and make consistent progress toward our goals. Success begets success. Each small accomplishment can give us momentum and motivation to keep going.

Harnessing available resources is key when starting on your journey to make your dreams come true. Resources include personal connections, financial aid, or industry knowledge. By tapping into your network, you could get valuable insights about the field you're interested in, helping you be successful in the long run.

Creating a detailed action plan is also a must. This plan should be specific and actionable enough so you can monitor your progress and make adjustments if needed. Access to adequate resources can be a game-changer when achieving success and living a fulfilling life. It gives us confidence, stability, and motivation, making it a reality. Taking action is up to you. That's the power of the YEARN advantage. Resources can be a powerful ally.

In business, resources are vital for companies to acquire the materials and tools they need to function. Resources come in many forms, and the economic climate affects how they can be accessed. Systems markets are exchanges of goods and services between businesses. The availability of resources can impact a company's competitiveness. Fiscal policies and systems play a significant role in how companies fund their operations.

When making decisions, the availability of resources must be taken into account. Companies need to be able to get the materials and tools they need for their production and R&D projects. To ensure the smooth running of operations, companies must find trustworthy vendors that provide quality resources at affordable prices and deliver on time. It is important to consider these factors when making decisions to achieve optimal cost and steady resource supply.

Beyond business, there are plenty of ways to use our resources: non-profits always seek donated resources. Get involved with an organization that supports something you believe in. Donations are another way to contribute, including crowdfunding campaigns.

Your time is a resource you can donate. Volunteering is a great way to give back and meet new people.

REVIEW Question for 'RESOURCES'

• What do you need to do it?

Related to "ACT" Question: What do you want to do?

N - Who do you Love?

*Who are the most SUPPORTIVE and INSPIRING
PEOPLE in your life, and how do they contribute to
your growth and well-being?*

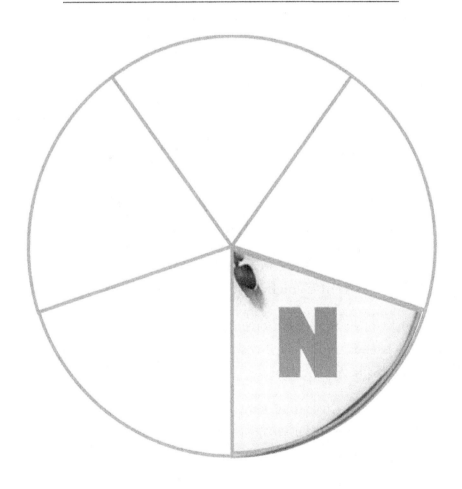

NETWORKS
IS CORE VALUE #5

"Network with people to collaborate and bring forth higher creativity on the path to greatness!"

We started with the first core value: YOU
We end with the fifth and final core value: Networks

Networks of People. Relationships come first. Relationships with family, friends, colleagues, coworkers, community alliances, and social network connections.

Relating to the previous core value, Resources, people are as valuable and essential to businesses as intangible resources of capital, technology, and equipment. That's why people are often called "Human Resources."

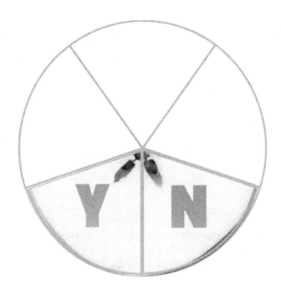

Humans matter. Relationships matter. Networks matter.

Your relationship with yourself is essential for building positive relationships with others. Address any underlying issues or insecurities within yourself. Then you can develop self-acceptance which leads to better relationships with.

The 'last' value, Network, is all about people. We started YEARN with 'You' and come full circle with 'Networks.' It starts and ends with people.

In 2011, a fire destroyed Richard Branson's house on his private Necker Island during Hurricane Irene. Celebrity actress, Kate Winslet, was one of about 20 people present during the fire. Despite the tragedy, there is a positive takeaway concerning the importance of people in this story.

Said Kate Winslet, a guest of Branson's at the time of the fire: "I will never forget Richard placing his arms around both my children as we were watching the flames, and saying, *'At the end of the day, what you realize is that all that matters is the people that you love. Everything else is just stuff. And none of that stuff matters.'"*

Questions for 'Networks'

- **What conversation(s) do you want to be in?**
- **Who do you want to associate with?**

Network - Build a Support System

The 'Networks' core value of the YEARN Advantage highlights the importance of people. Individuals and communities who help and enable your actions. To build a support system, consider the following questions:

- Who can support me in achieving this goal?

- Who has achieved similar goals before and can offer guidance and advice?

- Who can hold me accountable and keep me motivated?

- Are any communities or groups that share my goal and offer support?

Creating a support system is crucial in achieving your goals. It involves surrounding yourself with positive individuals who can provide guidance, motivation, and accountability. Being part of a community of like-minded individuals can contribute to your success and provide a sense of belonging and motivation.

Having a solid network of supportive people can positively impact your well-being. Friends and family who listen and offer kind words can reduce stress and boost self-confidence. Having someone in your life who genuinely cares about you is helpful when facing challenging personal situations. A supportive person allows for the safe processing of emotions, leading to improved mental health over time. Additionally, a supportive network can encourage physical health by providing motivation and understanding.

Interpersonal Relationships: Build mutual benefit and trust relationships, seeking outcomes that benefit all parties. Listen and empathize with others to build understanding and rapport.

Collaboration and Innovation: Leverage differences and work together to create innovative solutions that benefit all stakeholders. Innovation requires courage, not just brains. Use your tenacity, creativity, and teamwork. Step out of your comfort zone and have the courage to take risks.

Kindness: We all want to be treated with kindness and respect, starting with extending the same to others. Heartfelt actions involve showing empathy, compassion, and understanding toward others, even under difficult situations. This can involve simple acts of kindness like holding the door open for someone, offering a listening ear, or more significant actions like volunteering or donating to charity.

An ability to connect: As social creatures, we all crave connection and belonging. Build meaningful relationships with others. Listen attentively, show empathy, and find common ground. It also means being vulnerable and sharing our experiences and struggles, which can help build trust and understanding.

Loving: Love is a fundamental human emotion that brings us joy, fulfillment, and connection with others. Love can take many forms, including romantic, familial, and love for our friends and community. By cultivating loving relationships, we can experience a sense of belonging and purpose that enriches our lives.

Leaving a legacy: Leaving a legacy involves making a positive impact on the world and leaving behind a meaningful contribution that will endure beyond our lifetime. This can include contributing to our community through volunteer work, philanthropy, or other acts of service. It can also include pursuing a career or passion that helps others or positively impacts the environment or society. We can feel a sense of fulfillment and purpose by leaving a legacy, knowing that our lives have positively impacted the world.

Networks & Relationships: Develop positive and healthy relationships with the people in your life, whether your spouse, family members, friends, or even strangers. The people we surround ourselves with can significantly impact our thoughts, behaviors, and success. Surrounding ourselves with supportive, knowledgeable, and ambitious individuals can inspire us to become our best selves. Building positive relationships with people who can help us grow and achieve our goals is crucial in both personal and professional life.

A wider network means having connections or relationships with more people, both online and in person. Being part of a network lets us learn, collaborate, and develop. For instance, joining a professional organization can help us connect with others in our field, access valuable resources, and learn new skills.

6 Degrees of Networks

The "Six Degrees of Separation" theory suggests that any two people on earth connect through a chain of no more than six people. This is based on the idea that, on average, people tend to have a network of about 150 acquaintances. Through acquaintances, they are indirectly connected to everyone else in the world. The original experiments were performed in the late 1960s by psychologist Stanley Milgram. Kevin Bacon's celebrity made the "6 degrees of separation" a household concept.

For example, suppose you wanted to contact a particular celebrity or business leader. You may start by contacting someone in your network who knows that person, and then that person may know someone closer to the target, and so on. You can quickly reach your target by following the chain of connections within a few steps.

Social media and networking sites have made the "Six Degrees of Separation" more accessible. Social media enables people to expand their networks and connect with others only a few degrees away.

Your relationships are the aspect of you that touches the hearts of others. Connection is where the bonds are strengthened.

Our networks of people are intertwined through shared beliefs and norms that create a culture within a society or community. These cultures are how we live in our homes and in our workplaces and include language, religion, education, art, and other customs.

Culture can have a powerful influence on how people live their lives. It helps establish societal roles and determine how they communicate with others. These networks of many types of relationships can shape our behaviors and attitudes. Our relationships also have an impact on our physical and psychological health. People living in various societies may be exposed to multiple health issues due to cultural differences.

Here are three ways culture can affect how we network with others:

1. Language reveals our culture and affects our thinking and communication.

2. Religion: Religious beliefs shape our values and behaviors, often influencing our views on gender roles or same-sex marriage.

3. Education: Our educational systems reflect the values of our cultures, teaching us about history, politics, science, and more.

Humans are social creatures and our connections with others are essential to our well-being and sense of belonging.

Our identity, values, and beliefs are significantly formed by our nuclear family, including parents, siblings, and children. They provide us with emotional support, guidance, and a sense of belonging, influencing our socialization and development of essential communication and social skills.

Our extended family, including grandparents, aunts, uncles, and cousins, also plays a role in our cultural identity and traditions. Friends and colleagues are other important sources of social and emotional support that can direct our goals, careers, and well-being. Clubs, organizations, and religious groups provide opportunities to connect with like-minded individuals, develop new interests, and contribute to a larger community. They can also give a sense of purpose and meaning to our lives.

Our networks of people provide essential support, guidance, belonging, and purpose, enabling us to thrive as individuals and as a society.

Expanding Your Network

It's essential to be intentional about the networks we participate in and the relationships we build. Meeting with like-minded people can expand our knowledge and lead to new collaborations. Online forums and industry events provide opportunities to network, learn about trends, and stay updated.

Connecting with others online is a great way to build a support system and share experiences in a safe environment. Virtual platforms provide opportunities for socialization and networking.

Social media makes it easy to explore different networks and join groups related to your interests or values. This is particularly helpful when in-person meetings aren't possible due to safety concerns. You can join discussion forums, follow peers, and gain knowledge from experts. Virtual support groups provide a safe place to express yourself without judgment. Joining online communities can offer a supportive space to seek advice and connect with like-minded people who understand what you're going through.

Online platforms can help us stay connected even when we are physically apart, which has been crucial during uncertain times like the Covid-19 pandemic. They allow individuals to come together easily without leaving their homes. However, while online networks are useful, they offer a different level of intimacy than face-to-face interactions. Therefore, it is still important to participate in events and activities to meet and connect with others in person, as this can lead to deeper and more meaningful relationships and opportunities for collaboration and growth.

> *"Networking is simply the cultivating of mutually beneficial, give and take, win-win relationships. It works best when emphasizing the "give" part."*
> ~Bob Burg

Improve Communication Q&A

Clear and effective communication is crucial in both personal and professional settings. Prepare well-thought-out questions and answers. This shows respect for the other person and builds stronger connections based on mutual understanding and trust. Communication is essential for building strong relationships and networking effectively.

How do you ASK better questions?
How do you better RESPOND to various questions?

Here are some practical tips to improve your questioning, and if you are being asked, here are some ways to respond:

- ○ **ASK OPEN-ENDED QUESTIONS:** Open-ended questions require more than a simple yes or no response. They encourage the other person to share their thoughts and opinions in greater detail. Examples of open-ended questions include "What do you think about this situation?" and "Can you tell me more about your experience with this issue?"

How to Answer Open-Ended Questions:

- Be honest and authentic: When answering open-ended questions, your response must be honest and genuine. Share your thoughts and opinions in a way that is true to your perspective.

- Provide details and examples: Open-ended questions invite more detailed and informative responses, so provide specific information and examples to illustrate your points. This will help to enrich your answer and give a complete picture of your thoughts or experiences.

- Stay focused: While open-ended questions allow for more exploration, staying focused and relevant to the question is essential. Avoid rambling or going off on tangents that don't relate to the question.

- Listen actively: If the open-ended question is part of a conversation, listen to the other person's response and ask follow-up questions to explore their thoughts and perspectives further and help build a deeper understanding and connection between them.

o **AVOID LEADING QUESTIONS:** Leading questions can influence or bias the other person's response. To avoid leading questions, ask neutrally-phrased questions and avoid words that suggest a particular answer. For instance, instead of asking, "Don't you think this is the best solution?" ask, "What do you think is the best solution?"

How to Answer Leading Questions

When answering leading questions, it's essential to be aware of the bias or assumption embedded in the question. Avoid simply agreeing or disagreeing with the question.

Question: "Don't you think this is the best solution?"

Response: "I understand why you might think that, but I'm not sure it's the only solution. In my opinion, we should consider other possible solutions before making a final decision. Can I share some of those alternatives with you?"

By acknowledging the bias in the question and offering your perspective, you can clarify your position while respecting the other person's point of view. This type of response encourages further discussion and exploration of alternative solutions rather than simply accepting the initial assumption presented in the question.

o **BE SPECIFIC:** Specific questions focus on details and encourage more detailed and informative responses. Instead of asking a broad question like "What do you do?" ask a more specific question like "What are your primary responsibilities in your current role?"

Here are Some Tips for Answering Non-Specific Questions Effectively:

- Be clear and concise: When answering a non-specific question, your response must be clear and concise. Avoid providing unnecessary details or tangents that don't relate to the question. For example, you could respond to "What do you do?" by saying, "I work as a software engineer."

- Provide context: If the question is ambiguous or unclear, you can provide additional context to help clarify the question. For example, you could respond to "What do you do?" by saying, "Are you asking about my occupation or my hobbies?"

- Highlight your skills and achievements: When answering a non-specific question about your occupation or role, you can highlight your skills and accomplishments to provide a complete picture of what you do. For example, you could say, "I work as a software engineer and specialize in developing mobile applications."

- Ask for clarification: If you are uncertain about what the other person is asking, you can ask for clarification to better understand the intent behind the question. For example, you could say, "Can you be more specific about what you're asking?"

- o **KEEP IT CONCISE:** Lengthy questions can be challenging to understand and may lose the other person's attention. Keep your questions concise by focusing on one topic or idea at a time.

Examples of How to Ask the Other Person If They Want a Short or Long Answer:

- "Would you like a brief overview or a more detailed explanation?"

- "Are you looking for a quick answer, or do you want me to go into more detail?"

- "I can give you a short answer or longer answer with more detail. Which one would you prefer?"

- "Do you have a specific aspect you'd like me to focus on, or would you like a more general answer?"

- o **ASK FOLLOW-UP QUESTIONS:** Follow-up questions show active listening and are essential for effective communication. They clarify or expand on the information provided, including "Could you give me an example of what you mean?" and "How does that compare to your previous experience?" They can also create clarity when answering a question.

Keep these in mind to become a better communicator and enhance your ability to ask practical questions. Effective questioning and response skills are crucial for gathering information, building relationships, and gaining deeper insights into a particular topic.

A Note on Bias

The concept of bias has been mentioned several times. We read how leading questions can influence or bias the other person's response.

Two books to consider exploring bias are, *Thinking Fast and Slow,* by Daniel Kahneman and, *The 25 Cognitive Biases,* by Charles Munger. In Thinking Fast and Slow, Kahneman explains cognitive biases that affect our decision-making processes. He argues that System 1 thinking, which is fast and automatic, can be prone to biases like confirmation bias and availability bias. These biases can lead to errors in judgment and decision-making.

In *Thinking Fast and Slow*, Kahneman explains how our brains have two modes of thinking: System 1 (fast and intuitive) and System 2 (slow and analytical). He discusses how biases can affect our thinking. Bias includes confirmation bias (seeking information that confirms our beliefs) and availability bias (overestimating the importance of readily available information). Kahneman shows how these biases can lead to judgment and decision-making errors by focusing on the cognitive processes that cause them.

In *The 25 Cognitive Biases*, Munger identifies cognitive biases that impact our decision-making. The book lists biases such as confirmation bias, availability bias, and hindsight bias. Munger discusses the sunk cost fallacy, where people continue to invest resources in a project or decision because of their past investment, even if it no longer makes sense. This book is helpful for business people and investors, as it highlights the impact of these biases on financial decisions.

Finding Advisors, Coaches, Mentors

To succeed in your career or project, you need a support system of mentors and advisors. With the right people, you can leverage their experience to navigate obstacles. To find a mentor, be honest about your goals and the knowledge you need. Network beyond your inner circle, attend seminars, conferences, or online forums. A mentor can offer insight into areas where you lack experience, helping you achieve your goals more quickly.

Consider reaching out to professionals in your industry or academic field who can provide a fresh perspective and help you identify potential blind spots. Building relationships with advisors can also lead to new opportunities and connections that can help you advance in your career or achieve success in your project.

> *"Aim to make other people successful. And if you do that, the business will ultimately be more successful."*
> ~Mindy Grossman

Propinquity and Interpersonal Attraction

Propinquity means the closeness between people or things, either in physical or psychological terms. The similarity in nature or beliefs can also increase propinquity. The mere-exposure effect explains how repeated contact with a person or stimulus can create positive feelings and familiarity, even if initial feelings were neutral or negative.

Propinquity can also refer to the concept of kinship or familial relationships. People related by blood or marriage are said to have a high degree of propinquity, which can influence their behavior towards each other. For example, siblings or cousins may have a stronger bond and feel more comfortable around each other than they would with strangers.

People tend to be attracted to others who are similar to themselves. Propinquity can significantly impact human behavior and relationships. People tend to be more attracted to those who share similar traits, interests, and beliefs or who are in close proximity to them. This can lead to the forming of close relationships and social groups based on shared attitudes and worldviews.

How to Rekindle Old Connections

Reaching out to reconnect with former contacts can be intimidating, especially if you last interacted some time ago. The key is to make sure it's a positive experience for both parties. Start by personalizing your message and catching up on what's happened in the other person's life since you last spoke. People appreciate when you take the time to remember details about them and their journey.

Be vulnerable and explain why you're reaching out or what motivated you to reconnect. This will help create an atmosphere of trust and understanding, allowing for a more meaningful conversation. Ask thoughtful questions that show you are genuinely interested in hearing from them.

After the initial conversation, arrange follow-up meetings or calls so your relationship can continue growing. If the contact is somewhere other than local, suggest scheduling video calls or phone calls, depending on their preference. Show appreciation for any advice they've given or the help they have provided during your interaction. Rekindling old connections is possible if both of you are interested in maintaining the relationship.

Maintaining Your Support System

Once you have established a network of supportive individuals, it is vital to maintain that support system. The key is to nurture the relationships by staying connected and making time for one another.

Start by scheduling regular check-ins with your friends and family members. Connecting online or through video calls is a great way to stay updated on each other's lives and stay in touch. It's also important to be available when someone reaches out to you, so be sure to respond promptly and show that you care.

Make an effort to spend quality time together whenever possible. Even though it might not always be easy, try scheduling regular meetups with your friends or family members, even if it's just for an hour or two at a time. Not only will this help strengthen your relationships, but it will also give you something to look forward to during tough times.

When life gets hectic, don't forget the importance of those support systems. Cultivating solid connections with those around you is essential for physical and mental health. Take the necessary steps to build and preserve meaningful relationships with those who care most about you.

Strategies for Making Lasting Connections

Making meaningful connections with others is integral to building a solid support system. To do this, there are some key strategies to keep in mind.

The first step is to be authentic and open when meeting new people. Presenting yourself as you are is essential, without pretense or false impressions. When talking with someone, be honest about your feelings and experiences and listen intently to the other person's point of view. This will help build trust which creates a solid foundation for your relationships.

Participating in activities that promote deeper connections with others is essential. Examples include joining groups or clubs, attending events or classes, and hosting dinners with friends. Seeking new opportunities by connecting with like-minded individuals on social media, joining relevant organizations, or attending conferences can also lead to valuable relationships. Building positive relationships and expanding our networks can provide personal and professional growth opportunities.

"The only way to have a friend is to be one."
~Ralph Waldo Emerson

YOU, Relationships and Greatness

Greatness in a person's growth can found the domain of relationships.

Personal development involves individual efforts and also affects our relationships. How we interact with others can shape our beliefs and attitudes, ultimately influencing our self-growth.

"We've found that the influence of your friends and people you have connections with can affect your health just as much as your family history or your genetic background," says Nicholas Christakis, professor of medicine at Harvard.

The Grant Study is a research project from the late 1930s at Harvard University that tracked 268 male Harvard undergraduates from their sophomore year in college for over 80 years. Researchers regularly interviewed, surveyed, and examined the participants to collect information on their physical health, career, social relationships, and psychological well-being.

After years of analyzing the data, the longtime director of the study George Vaillant, said, ***"That the only thing that really matters in life are your relationships with other people."***

Vaillant concluded that the most crucial factor in leading a happy and fulfilling life is the quality of one's relationships with others. Participants who reported having close and supportive relationships with family and friends were more likely to be happy, healthy, and successful, had fewer health problems, and were more likely to live longer.

When we engage in relationships with others, we are forced to confront our limitations, biases, and shortcomings. Interactions with others can increase empathy, compassion, and understanding by exposing us to different perspectives. Relationships provide opportunities for self-improvement as we receive feedback and support from others.

Furthermore, a person's character is cultivated in relationships. Our character is reflected in our actions, attitudes, and behaviors toward others. Our relationships can either improve or diminish our character traits. For example, we are more likely to develop positive character traits if we consistently act toward others with integrity and kindness.

The accurate measure of a person's growth and greatness is found in the domain of relationships. To measure personal growth, we should look at how our relationships with others reflect our character development and positive impact. Greatness should not be measured solely by individual achievements, but also by the cumulative positive impact we have on those around us and the world as a whole.

REVIEW Questions for 'NETWORKS'

- **What conversation(s) do you want to be in?**

- **With whom do you want to associate?**

Sherrie's Motto:
'The Real Currency is Relationship Riches.'

PART
III

Mastery and The YEARN Advantage

When you improve one area of the YEARN advantage, it will ripple through all the others. Making changes in one aspect of your life can positively affect other areas.

Imagine yourself standing on the banks of a still lake, the water's surface reflecting the blue sky above. You hold a small pebble and toss it into the water with a flick of your wrist.

The pebble hits the surface, creating a small splash, and ripples spread out in all directions, moving further from the point of impact. The ripples grow wider and weaker as they travel, eventually fading altogether.

Now imagine that the pebble is a positive change in your life, such as starting a new exercise routine or taking a course to learn a new skill. At first, the difference may seem small, just like the splash of the pebble hitting the water. But just as the ripples from the pebble spread out in all directions, so will the effects of your positive change spread throughout your life.

As you start to exercise regularly, you may notice that you have more energy throughout the day. This newfound energy might inspire you to take up a new hobby or spend more time with your loved ones. Or, as you learn a new skill, you may feel more confident and capable in other areas of your life.

Positive changes can have a ripple effect, leading to unexpected benefits. For instance, regular exercise not only improves physical health but also boosts energy and mood. This can translate into increased productivity at work and improved relationships with loved ones. Starting small and focusing on incremental improvements in one area can have a domino effect on other areas of life. Whether it's improving physical health, exploring new hobbies, or working on personal development, every positive change can have far-reaching impacts.

Focus on incremental improvements in one area of the YEARN advantage. Every positive change you make can have a ripple effect that improves other areas of your life, whether improving your physical health, taking up a new hobby, or working on self-development.

So, feel free to take that first step, no matter how small it may seem. The ripples you create may change your life in ways you never imagined.

Mastery of the five values of the YEARN advantage puts you in charge of the direction of your life.

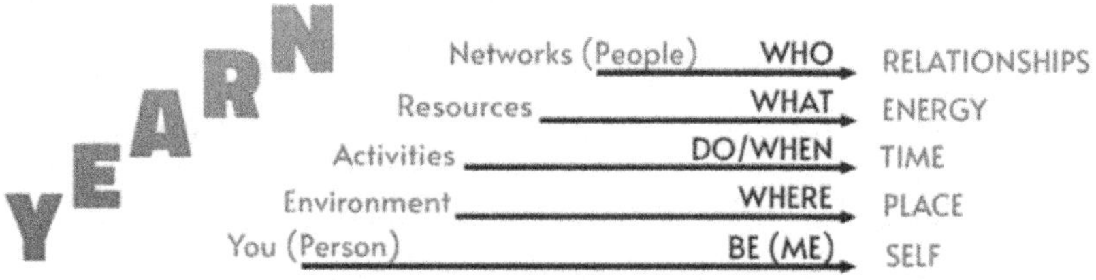

Figure 2 YEARN Core Stack

What is Mastery?

MASTERY refers to achieving a high level of knowledge, skill, and expertise in a particular area. It involves deep proficiency to apply yourself creatively.

To achieve mastery, putting in the time and focused attention is essential. It's not just about reaching a goal - it's about pursuing a learning process and honing your skills. Mastery is a journey, a lifelong passionate pursuit of continuous improvement and growth. There's always room to grow, and it's all about honing your skills and taking them to the next level on the path to greatness.

Becoming a master in your craft requires a combination of natural talent, effort, perseverance, and a growth mindset. It involves taking risks, making mistakes, and learning from failure. Mastery means becoming really good at something to the point where it becomes easy and allows you to be creative and innovative. To achieve mastery, one needs to be disciplined, set high standards, constantly improve skills, and be adaptable to new challenges.

In the pursuit of mastery, it is also essential to cultivate a sense of curiosity and openness to new experiences and perspectives. This involves seeking diverse viewpoints, exploring new ideas, and experimenting with different approaches.

ACHIEVING GREATNESS

Achieving greatness is a lofty desire, but it is not impossible. With the right combination of factors, anyone can reach their full potential and accomplish amazing things.

Self-discipline is crucial in achieving success and can be more critical than talent alone. It involves controlling your behavior and emotions while working towards your goals. With self-discipline, you can work hard, overcome obstacles, and maintain focus on your objectives, even in challenging situations.

The importance of self-discipline in achieving success is highlighted in the saying "Self-discipline without talent can often achieve astounding results." Conversely, "talent without self-discipline inevitably dooms itself to failure." While talent is important, more than talent alone is needed to succeed.

Both talent and self-discipline are essential factors in achieving success. While some people may be naturally talented, self-discipline is a skill anyone can learn and develop. It may be the critical factor that determines whether you succeed or fail.

Achieving greatness can vary from person to person. Some universal factors are crucial in attaining greatness. Here are some of the most critical factors:

It starts with having a clear vision of what you want to achieve is crucial. See more in the chapter, *Activate Enhavim*. Visualizing an image gives you direction and purpose, helping you focus your actions toward achieving your desired outcome. Whether starting a business or pursuing a career in the arts, a clear vision can help you stay focused and motivated.

Your mindset is another critical factor. Use essential traits that help you stay dedicated to your goals. Activate passion, enthusiasm, perseverance, resilience, continuous learning, and accept failure. A positive and empowered mindset can help you overcome obstacles and achieve great things.

The environment you are in can also have a significant impact on your success. Access to resources such as funding, technology, and education can also make a big difference. As an athlete, having access to excellent training facilities, coaches, and equipment can give you an advantage.

Of course, effort and dedication are essential to achieving greatness. There is no shortcut to success; you must put in the effort and be committed to achieve your dreams.

Achieving greatness requires a clear vision, the right mindset, necessary resources, a supportive environment, and a network of mentors. Being around positive and supportive people can encourage and challenge you to be your best self, and help you overcome obstacles. With these factors in place, anyone can achieve their full potential and accomplish amazing things.

MASTERY AND THE YEARN CORE VALUES

Personal Development: (Y) Mastering personal development involves continually learning, growing, and pursuing your passions and interests. Here are some examples:

- Setting and achieving meaningful goals.

- Seeking out new experiences that challenge you and broaden your perspective.

- Developing a growth mindset and embracing challenges and setbacks as opportunities for learning and improvement.

- Cultivating the physical, emotional, mental intelligence, and spiritual path to higher self-awareness helps you understand yourself and others better.

- Pursuing hobbies and interests that bring you joy and fulfillment.

Health and Wellness: (Y) Mastering your health and wellness requires creating and maintaining healthy habits that support your physical and mental well-being. Here are some examples:

- Eating a balanced diet provides your body with the nutrients it needs.

- Engaging in regular physical activity that strengthens your body and mind.

- Managing stress through relaxation techniques and self-care practices.

- Prioritizing quality sleep to allow your body to rest and recover.

- Being mindful of your health and proactively seeking medical care when necessary.

- Avoid unhealthy habits like smoking, excessive alcohol consumption, and drug use.

Environmental Factors (E): Mastering environmental factors involves creating and maintaining living spaces, digital realms, sustainable communities, supportive work, recreational environments, and safe spaces promoting physical and mental well-being. Here are some examples:

- *Natural environment mastery:* Knowledge of environmental issues and practices promoting sustainability and biodiversity.

  - Develop and implement sustainable practices within your organization and personal life.

  - Collaborate with environmental experts and organizations to identify opportunities for improvement.

- *Built environment mastery:* Stay current with building codes and rules that offer accessibility, safety, and energy efficiency.

  - Invest in technologies and infrastructure that improve the built environment.

  - Collaborate with architects and engineers to design buildings and infrastructure that prioritize safety, functionality, and sustainability.

- *Digital environment mastery:* Stay informed about digital trends and potential online threats.

  - Develop and enforce policies and guidelines that promote responsible online behavior.

  - Engage in ongoing education and training to stay current with the evolving digital landscape.

- *Social environment mastery:* Develop and implement initiatives that foster community building and promote diversity and inclusivity.

  - Provide training and resources to help individuals develop positive social skills and behaviors.

  - Collaborate with community leaders and organizations to identify opportunities for improvement.

- *Economic environment mastery:* Develop and implement policies and initiatives that promote equitable distribution of wealth and resources.

  - Engage in community development initiatives that prioritize economic sustainability and social responsibility.

  - Invest in education and job training programs to improve employment opportunities.

- *Political environment mastery:* Advocate for policies that promote social justice and human rights.

  - Develop and implement initiatives that increase civic engagement and participation.

  - Hold elected officials accountable for their actions and decisions.

Mastery of environmental factors requires ongoing learning, collaboration, and action. Individuals and organizations can create supportive environments that promote well-being by prioritizing sustainable practices, promoting inclusivity and diversity, and advocating for social justice.

Act as an Entrepreneur: (A) Major actions you can take to achieve mastery and success:

A. *Develop a deep understanding of your industry:* Stay informed about industry trends, changes, and best practices. Research and analyze your competition to identify areas for improvement and opportunities for growth.

B. *Set clear goals:* Develop specific, measurable goals that align with your enhavim vision and strategy. Monitor your progress regularly and adjust your approach as needed.

C. *Embrace innovation:* Use creativity to stay ahead of the competition. Encourage experimentation and risk-taking within your team, and be open to new ideas and approaches.

D. *Employ technology:* Use technology to your advantage. Stay current with the latest tools and software that can help you streamline your operations, improve efficiency, and enhance customer experience.

E. *Apply continuous learning:* Commit to continuous learning by attending workshops, webinars, and conferences. Read industry publications and books, and seek feedback from mentors and colleagues.

F. *Build a strong team and partnerships:* Hire talented individuals who share your vision and values. Delegate responsibilities and provide ongoing training and support to help your team members grow and develop. Connect with suppliers, vendors, and other businesses to expand your reach and access new opportunities.

G. *Focus on customer satisfaction*: Prioritize customer satisfaction by providing high-quality products or services, delivering exceptional customer service, and continually seeking feedback to improve your offerings.

Employees can adopt an entrepreneurial mindset by taking ownership of their work, proactively seeking opportunities to add value, and developing innovative solutions. They can also expand their skills and knowledge beyond their current roles by seeking training and development opportunities and building relationships. Being adaptable and flexible in their approach to work is also important, as it helps drive the organization forward and positions employees as valuable contributors to its success.

Individual employees can act like entrepreneurs within their organization by adopting an entrepreneurial mindset, developing their skills and knowledge, and being adaptable and flexible in their approach to work. Employees can position themselves for success and enhance their professional reputation by doing so.

RESOURCES & Financial Stability: (R) Mastering your finances involves being mindful of your spending habits and creating and following a budget that aligns with your goals and values. Here are some examples:

A. Managing debt effectively.

B. Investing wisely for the future.

C. Avoiding unnecessary expenses and planning for emergencies and unexpected expenses.

D. Creating a financial plan that allows you to pursue the things that matter most to you without the burden of financial stress.

NETWORK Your Relationships: (N) Mastering your relationships involves developing strong interpersonal skills and building healthy connections with the important people in your life. Here are some examples:

A. Developing effective communication, empathy, active listening, and conflict resolution skills.

B. Building and maintaining healthy relationships with family, friends, and romantic partners.

C. Investing time and effort into creating meaningful connections.

D. Being supportive, reliable, and trustworthy.

E. Showing appreciation and gratitude for those in your life.

By mastering these essential skills, you can build a more rewarding, purposeful, and prosperous life based on well-being, contentment, and self-improvement. Though acquiring these abilities might require dedication and perseverance, the rewards are priceless.

Entrepreneur's Business Mastery

Next are vital areas to master in business:

Leadership: Mastering practical leadership skills is crucial for guiding and motivating your team toward achieving your business goals. Here are some examples:

A. Setting clear objectives and expectations.

B. Delegating tasks and responsibilities effectively.

C. Providing constructive feedback and recognition.

D. Fostering a positive work culture that encourages collaboration, innovation, and growth.

E. Leading by example and modeling the behavior you expect from others.

Marketing and Sales: Mastering marketing and sales strategies are essential for growing and scaling a successful business. Here are some examples:

A. Identifying and understanding your target audience.

B. Developing a solid brand identity that sets your business apart from competitors.

C. Creating effective marketing campaigns that resonate with your audience.

D. Building relationships with customers and maintaining their loyalty.

E. Staying up-to-date with industry trends, competition, and adapting to changes in the market.

Financial Management: Mastering financial management skills ensure your business's long-term success and sustainability. Here are some examples:

A. Creating and managing budgets that align with your business goals.

B. Forecasting financial performance and identifying areas for improvement.

C. Managing cash flow effectively ensures your business has the resources to operate and grow.

D. Understanding financial statements and using them to make informed business decisions.

E. Seeking advice from financial experts and professionals when necessary.

Innovation: Mastering innovative thinking and problem-solving skills is essential for staying ahead of the competition and identifying new opportunities for growth and expansion. Here are some examples:

A. Keeping abreast of industry trends and advancements.

B. Identifying and anticipating changes in the market.

C. Encouraging creativity and experimentation within your team.

D. Being open to new ideas and perspectives.

E. Taking calculated risks to pursue new growth opportunities.

Creating a Positive Business Culture: Mastering the art of creating a positive business culture is essential for building an engaged, motivated, and committed team for your business. Here are some examples:

A. Developing a clear set of core principles that guide your business practices and decision-making.
B. Creating a supportive and inclusive work environment that values diversity and promotes equality.
C. Encouraging open communication and feedback among team members.
D. Recognizing and rewarding employees for their hard work and contributions.
E. Providing opportunities for professional development and growth.

By becoming proficient and mastering these important areas, you can set your business up for sustained success and expansion while fostering a pleasant and rewarding work atmosphere for yourself and your colleagues. Though honing these skills will require dedication and hard work, the rewards are well worth the effort.

YEARN in Review

Yes, this title is a play on "Year in Review."

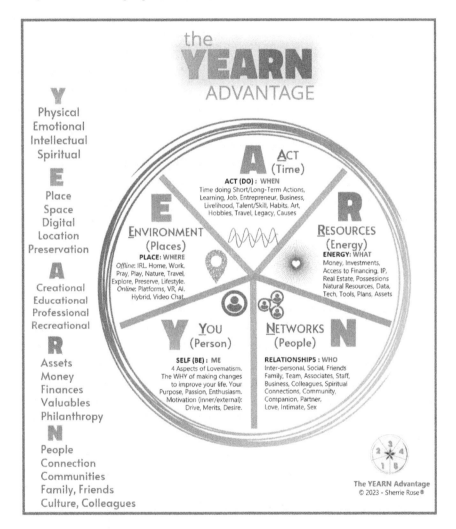

the
YEARN
ADVANTAGE

Y
Physical
Emotional
Intellectual
Spiritual

E
Place
Space
Digital
Location
Preservation

A
Creational
Educational
Professional
Recreational

R
Assets
Money
Finances
Valuables
Philanthropy

N
People
Connection
Communities
Family, Friends
Culture, Colleagues

A **ACT**
(Time)
ACT (DO) : WHEN
Time doing Short/Long-Term Actions,
Learning, Job, Entrepreneur, Business,
Livelihood, Talent/Skill, Habits, Art,
Hobbies, Travel, Legacy, Causes

E **ENVIRONMENT**
(Places)
PLACE: WHERE
Offline: IRL. Home, Work,
Pray, Play, Nature, Travel,
Explore, Preserve, Lifestyle.
Online: Platforms, VR, AI.
Hybrid, Video Chat.

R **RESOURCES**
(Energy)
ENERGY: WHAT
Money, Investments,
Access to Financing, IP,
Real Estate, Possessions
Natural Resources, Data,
Tech, Tools, Plans, Assets

Y **YOU**
(Person)
SELF (BE) : ME
4 Aspects of Lovematism.
The WHY of making changes
to improve your life. Your
Purpose, Passion, Enthusiasm.
Motivation (inner/external):
Drive, Merits, Desire.

N **NETWORKS**
(People)
RELATIONSHIPS : WHO
Inter-personal, Social, Friends
Family, Team, Associates, Staff,
Business, Colleagues, Spiritual
Connections, Community,
Companion, Partner,
Love, Intimate, Sex

The YEARN Advantage
© 2023 - Sherrie Rose®

Figure 3. The YEARN Advantage 'At-a-Glance'

Y.E.A.R.N. ADVANTAGE

"You can unlock your ambitions and strive for greatness - Harness Your Power!" (YOU)

"Encourage and nurture a space that motivates and energizes greatness!" (ENVIRONMENT)

"Act now and make it happen - Build the bridge between goals and greatness!" (ACT)

"Ramp up your resources; it's a great strategy with lasting rewards!" (RESOURCES)

"Network with people to collaborate and bring forth higher creativity on the path to greatness!" (NETWORKS)

YOU

YOU VALUE: The "You" in YEARN refers to your qualities, skills, and experiences in physical, emotional, intellectual, and spiritual aspects, including passions and expertise. By leveraging the five values of YEARN, individuals can achieve their goals and improve their lives.

It starts with YOU! You value who you are and what you can do.

Personal Agency:

- The ability to take control of one's own life and make choices that reflect one's values, goals, and desires.

- The ability to be true to oneself and live according to one's values and beliefs.

Self-worth and Self-esteem:

- o The belief that one is valuable and worthy of love and respect, regardless of factors such as achievement or status.

Personal Fulfillment and Happiness:

- o The experience of joy, satisfaction, and meaning in life.

Authenticity and Personal Identity:

- o The ability to be true to oneself and live according to one's values and beliefs.

Personal Accountability and Responsibility:

- o Set reasonable expectations for your progress and growth.

- o Hold yourself accountable for your progress and take responsibility for your actions. Reflect on your progress and identify areas where you need to improve.

Self-Care and Sleep:

- o Practice self-care to care for yourself physically, mentally, and emotionally.

- o Get enough sleep each night to maintain your ability to concentrate and focus.

Growth Mindset:

- o The pursuit of personal and professional growth, learning, and development.

o Embrace challenges as opportunities to develop your skills and overcome obstacles.

o Accept failure as an opportunity to learn, adapt, and grow.

o Identify and address limiting beliefs to create a positive, supportive inner dialogue that boosts your confidence.

o See challenges and setbacks as opportunities for growth and learning rather than fixed limitations on your abilities or potential.

o Employ an empowered mindset that values effort, persistence, and continuous improvement.

Consistency and Resilience:

o Emphasize consistency over perfection and focus on making progress consistently over time.

o Take calculated risks that align with your goals and vision.

o Cultivate a positive attitude to stay motivated and focused on your goals.

o Engage perseverance to pursue your goals despite obstacles and setbacks.

o Develop resilience to bounce back from setbacks and keep moving forward.

o Practice self-reflection to identify your strengths and weaknesses, understand your motivations, and develop greater self-awareness.

Personal Traits:

o Develop qualities within yourself that help you achieve your goals, dreams, and enhavim.

o Embrace humility by acknowledging your imperfections and being open to learning from others.

o Foster curiosity by having a thirst for knowledge and exploring new things.

o Nurture creativity by thinking outside the box and finding innovative solutions to problems.

o Show courage by taking risks and facing your fears.

Developing personal traits like a positive attitude, proactivity, creativity, facing fears, taking risks, and building resilience can help you overcome challenges, pursue your dreams, and continuously improve and grow. These traits enable you to be proactive in your approach to problems, finding creative solutions. By stepping out of your comfort zone and taking risks, you expand your capabilities and resilience, which can serve you well in the future.

> *"Personal growth and increased confidence take place when we are testing the limits of our lives."*
> ~Thomas Payne, Inventor

ENVIRONMENT

ENVIRONMENT VALUE: The "Environment" in the YEARN advantage refers to the external factors influencing your ability to achieve your goals. This includes economic conditions, social and cultural norms, and digital and environmental factors.

Sense of Connection and Belonging to Your Physical Location:

o   The feeling of being rooted in a particular place and feeling a sense of connection and belonging to that place.

Inspiration and Awe from Your Surroundings:

o   The experience of being moved, inspired, or awed by the beauty and majesty of nature, the universe, or your physical surroundings.

Personal Growth and Discovery within Your Environment:

o The opportunity to learn, explore, and grow within the physical and online environments they inhabit.

Nostalgia and Sentimentality Towards Familiar Places:

o The emotional connection and attachment to familiar places and their associated memories.

Connection to Spirituality or the Divine within Your Environment:

o The connection to something greater than oneself, whether through nature, religion, or personal spiritual practice.

Positive Experiences within Online and Physical Environments:

o The ability to engage with others and have positive experiences within both online and physical environments.

Opportunities for Connection and Networking:

o The ability to connect with others, build relationships, and network within your physical or online communities.

Actions you can take to improve your various "environments"

Evaluate your current environment:

o Take a look at the people, places, and things in your life that may be hindering or supporting your growth and progress.

Create a supportive environment conducive to your goals:

o   Move or make changes at home or work. Perhaps choose to exercise in a gym instead of at home.

Keep your workspace clean:

o   Be organized, avoid clutter, and create a designated workspace.

Minimize distractions:

o   Identify and minimize any distractions in your physical, online, or mental environment that may be taking away from your focus and productivity. This could set boundaries with technology and social media or practice mindfulness and meditation to quiet your mind and improve your concentration. We can maximize our time by eliminating distractions and focusing on our priorities.

Online environment:

o   Pay attention to the content you consume online and the people you interact with on social media. Consider unfollowing or limiting your time with people or content that don't align with your goals and values.

By understanding and adapting to your environment, you can better position yourself to achieve greatness and make a positive impact.

ACT

ACT VALUE: "To Act" is the value in the YEARN advantage that refers to an individual's steps to achieve their goals. Taking intentional and practical actions, including planning, preparation, execution, ongoing learning, and improvement, can help individuals progress toward their goals and make a positive impact.

o *Take action:* Start the plan you have created and be consistent in your efforts to develop the skills, traits, habits, and mindset you need to achieve your goals.

o *Stay focused on your vision:* Keep your vision and goals in mind, and stay focused on them even when faced with setbacks or obstacles. See more in *Activate Enhavim* section.

o *Stay flexible:* Be willing to adjust your plan as needed.

o *Celebrate small wins*: Celebrate your progress and accomplishments, no matter how small.

o *Create accountability systems*: Establish accountability measures to keep yourself motivated. Set deadlines, track progress, and share your goals with others.

o   *Identify the skills*, traits, habits, and mindset you need: Know your enhavim and goals, identify the skills, traits, habits, and mindset. Start small and build up over time.

Simply stating or thinking positively about a task or goal without taking any action toward accomplishing it is not enough. Thinking or talking does not lead to the actual completion of the task.

Positive thinking and affirmations can help boost confidence, but concrete actions are necessary to achieve the desired results. "All talk and no action," refers to someone who talks about doing something but never takes steps to follow through.

To achieve a goal, it's essential to take action and make plans. Summoning resources and strategies involve actively seeking tools, knowledge, and skills and setting realistic steps toward accomplishing the task.

RESOURCES

RESOURCES VALUE: The "Resources" in the YEARN advantage are the things that people can use to achieve their goals, like money, tools, education, skills, and talents. By using these resources effectively, individuals can make the most of them and reach their objectives.

Identify the financial resources:

o Resources and tools needed to achieve your enhavim and goals.

Security and Stability:

o The feeling of safety and stability comes with having resources and assets that can provide for one's basic needs and future.

Independence and Autonomy:

o The ability to make choices and decisions not limited by financial constraints or dependence on others.

Status and Recognition:

o The achievement and recognition of owning assets and resources valued by society and others.

Generosity and Giving Back:

o The opportunity to use your resources and assets to help others and contribute to the greater good.

Opportunities and Experiences:

o The ability to pursue opportunities and experiences that may not be possible without the resources and assets that one possesses or has access to. This can include travel, education, and other life experiences that can enrich your life.

NETWORK

NETWORK VALUE: The "Network" in the YEARN advantage refers to the people and groups an individual is personally and professionally connected to. By building strong and supportive relationships with others, individuals can expand their influence and make a positive impact on a larger scale.

Love and Connection:

o The love and profound connections formed through relationships with family, friends, and others.

o Lovematism: the physical, mental, emotional, and spiritual bonds you experience with another person and with yourself. This includes the ability to manage your emotions and the emotional intimacy to connect on a deeper level.

o Communication: the ability to effectively communicate with others, including active listening and expressing your thoughts and feelings clearly.

o Active listening: being attentive and fully engaged in conversations, listening to understand rather than just waiting to respond.

o Empathy: the ability to understand and share the feelings of others and see things from their perspective, which can help foster deeper connections and relationships.

o Trust: the willingness to be vulnerable and rely on others and the ability to be trustworthy and reliable in return.

o Boundaries: the ability to set healthy boundaries in relationships, which helps ensure mutual respect and understanding.

o Forgiveness: the ability to forgive others and oneself, which can help repair damaged relationships and strengthen bonds.

o Altruism: the selfless concern for the well-being of others, which can foster stronger connections and relationships.

o Respectfulness: Treating others with dignity, respect, and kindness, regardless of their background.

o Gratitude: the regular practice of expressing gratitude for people, opportunity, or good fortune can foster a more profound sense of connection and appreciation.

"Love is the only way to grasp another human being in the innermost core of his personality."
~Viktor Frankl

Personal Growth and Development:

- o The ability to learn and grow through interactions and the support of friends, family members, mentors, and coaches.
- o Seek out new experiences and challenges to expand your knowledge and skills.
- o Continuously reflect on your thoughts and actions to identify areas for improvement.

Shared Goals and Values:

- o Look for opportunities to connect with others with similar interests, values, and goals.

Learn from others:

- o Seek out role models who have achieved similar goals and learn from their experiences.

Collaboration and Teamwork:

- o Working together towards a common goal, sharing skills, knowledge, and resources to achieve a shared objective.

Making a Positive Impact:

- o The opportunity to use your abilities and assets to assist others and positively impact society by helping your loved ones, engaging in volunteer work, or working toward a shared goal. On a large scale, to advance humanity.

Surround yourself with supportive people:

- Seek out individuals who inspire and motivate you to be your best self. Such as mentors or like-minded individuals who share your goals and can provide support and guidance.

Ask for feedback:

- Seek feedback from others to gain insights into your strengths and areas for growth and improvement.

Interpersonal Traits:

- Develop qualities in your interactions with others, such as gratitude, compassion, and joyfulness.
- Show kindness and empathy towards others to build strong relationships and meaningful connections.
- Being flexible, open-minded, and adaptable, willing to compromise and work with others to find solutions.
- Find joy in connecting with others to bring positivity to your interactions.
- Have a positive outlook on life to radiate joy and bring a sense of fun and playfulness to those around you.

Reviewing the YEARN Advantage, we have addressed these questions:

Y- **"Whose life is it anyway?"** raises the question of **YOU**, your autonomy and personal agency in the context of decision-making, and the right to self-determination for your life's direction.

E- **"Where does it take place?"** is a question about the **ENVIRONMENT,** such as physical or digital location, specific settings such as a home, workplace, or public spaces.

A- **"When does Action happen?"** refers to the timing of events or **ACTIONS**, ranging from immediate responses to ongoing processes or long-term plans.

R- **"What does Money have to do with it?"** is a question about the various forms of **RESOURCES** and money and other aspects such as access to assets, opportunities, and leveraging social status.

N- **"Who do you love?"** raises the topic of various **NETWORKS** of people we care for and work with, relationships, familial bonds, friendships, and professional and community connections.

The "Some" total of YEARN

- Someone to love (You, Networks)

- Something to do (Act)

- Somewhere to do it is (Environment)

- Some resources to do it (Resources)

- Something to look forward to (Your Dreams & Enhavim)

Stories That Personify YEARN

Next are five stories of individuals who personify the YEARN advantage:

Story 1: SOPHIA

Name: Sophia Kim *Age:* 28 *Location:* San Francisco, California

Sophia Kim always had a passion for baking, and after years of working as a pastry chef in various restaurants, she decided to start her bakery. With the help of her family and friends, Sophia was able to open her bakery in less than a year. She named it "Sweet Dreams Bakery" and started selling her delicious baked goods online.

Sophia's enhavim is to provide her customers with the best quality baked goods while maintaining an eco-friendly approach. Her mission is to create a bakery that satisfies the taste buds and contributes to the environment.

Sophia's YEARN advantage is her passion for baking (You), her use of organic and locally-sourced ingredients, as well as biodegradable packaging, to create a more sustainable business model (Environment), her commitment to creating a sustainable and scalable business model that can grow with her business (Actions), her family's funding of her venture, as well as access to specialized baking equipment and ingredients (Resources), her network of loyal customers, and partnerships with other local businesses and organizations, including her focus on building a solid online presence through social media and other digital channels (Network).

With her unique approach and delicious baked goods, Sophia's bakery quickly gained popularity and now has a loyal customer base. She is continuously expanding her business and has even started offering baking classes to share her passion and knowledge with others.

Story 2: ALEX

Name: Alex Rodriguez *Age:* 35 *Location:* Boston, Massachusetts

Alex Rodriguez is an avid runner who has always dreamed of running the Boston Marathon. He has been training for months and is finally preparing to participate in the race. Alex has always been competitive and loves the challenge of pushing himself to his limits.

Alex's enhavim is to push himself to achieve his dream while inspiring others to do the same. His mission is to promote a healthy and active lifestyle while setting an example for others.

Alex's YEARN advantage is his passion for running (You), his commitment to living a healthy lifestyle, including access to specialized training programs and coaches (Environment), his dedication to training and self-improvement (Actions), his access to the university's running track and other state-of-the-art athletic facilities (Resources), his network of fellow runners and fitness enthusiasts, including valuable partnerships with local running clubs and organizations (Network), and his ability to motivate and inspire others to adopt a healthy and active lifestyle.

On race day, Alex was ready to give it his all. He ran the entire race with determination and perseverance, even when he hit a wall at mile 20. With the support of his family and friends and the encouragement of fellow runners and spectators, Alex crossed the finish line with a smile on his face and a sense of accomplishment.

Alex's Boston Marathon experience has only strengthened his enhavim, and he continues to inspire others to pursue their own fitness goals. He now runs a fitness blog and regularly speaks at local schools and events, sharing his story and motivating others to live an active and healthy lifestyle.

Story 3: MARIA

Name: Maria Hernandez *Age:* 50 *Location:* Madrid, Spain

Maria Hernandez is a member of the International Olympic Committee (IOC). She has been a sports enthusiast and has always dreamed of being part of the Olympic movement. Maria's role in the IOC involves selecting and organizing venues for the Olympic Games.

Maria's enhavim is to promote the Olympic values of excellence, respect, and friendship while ensuring the success of the games. Her mission is to provide the best possible experience for athletes and spectators while promoting the positive impact of sports on society.

Maria's YEARN advantage is her love for sports (You), her focus on sustainable and inclusive practices, including access to specific training programs and cutting-edge equipment (Environment), her attention to detail and organizational skills (Actions), her membership in several sports professionals and organizations, with whom she has established valuable partnerships (Resources), and her ability to build relationships and collaborate with stakeholders, including athletes, coaches, and sport's governing bodies (Network).

Maria has had the opportunity to impact the Olympic movement significantly through her work in the IOC. She has selected and organized multiple Olympic Games, including the 2028 Summer Olympics, to be held in Los Angeles.

Maria's commitment to the Olympic values earned her respect and admiration from athletes, officials, and fans. She continues to work tirelessly to promote the Olympic movement and ensure the success of future games.

Story 4: JACK

Name: Jack Lee *Age:* 45 *Location:* Houston, Texas

Jack Lee is an aerospace engineer currently leading a team of engineers in developing a new space shuttle. Jack has always been passionate about space exploration and has worked on various projects.

Jack's enhavim is to advance space technology and exploration while ensuring the safety and success of space missions. His vision is to create a new space shuttle that is more efficient, reliable, and cost-effective than previous models.

Jack's YEARN advantage is his expertise in aerospace engineering (You) and access to cutting-edge technology. He is focused on creating sustainable and innovative space technology and partnerships with other companies and organizations in the industry (Environment), his attention to detail and quality control (Actions), his extensive education and experience in the space industry, including previous work on successful space shuttle projects (Resources), and his ability to lead and inspire his team, which includes skilled engineers, technicians, and support staff (Network).

The development of the new space shuttle has been a challenging process, but Jack and his team are making progress. Their unique design includes several improvements that make it safer and more efficient than previous models.

Jack is confident that their new space shuttle will significantly advance space exploration. He continues working tirelessly with his team to ensure the project's success and looks forward to the day their shuttle takes flight.

Story 5: SARAH

Name: Sarah Johnson *Age:* 30 *Location:* Los Angeles, California

Sarah Johnson is a social worker dedicated to solving the issue of homelessness in her city. She has seen firsthand the devastating effects of homelessness on individuals and families and is committed to solving the problem.

Sarah's enhavim is to create a world where everyone has a safe and stable place to call home. Her vision is to provide comprehensive services and support to individuals experiencing homelessness while advocating for policy changes that address the root causes of the problem.

Sarah's YEARN advantage is her empathy and compassion for others (You), her focus on addressing the root causes of homelessness, such as poverty and lack of affordable housing (Environment), her experience and expertise in social work (Actions), her connections with builders and suppliers who specialize in affordable housing and construction for non-profit organizations and grant funding she has secured for homeless assistance programs (Resources), her network of community organizations and volunteers, and her ability to collaborate with government officials and other stakeholders (Network).

Sarah has worked with various communities and non-profits to provide services such as shelter, food, and healthcare to those experiencing homelessness. She has also worked with local policymakers to advocate for increased funding for affordable housing and other programs to address homelessness.

Sarah's efforts have significantly impacted the issue of homelessness in her city. She has helped provide services and support to countless individuals and families, and her advocacy has increased awareness and action on the issue. Despite the challenges, Sarah remains committed to her enhavim and continues to work towards creating a world where everyone has a place to call home.

Through the Lens of YEARN

METAPHORICALY, a "lens" refers to a perspective or point of view used to interpret and understand an idea or concept.

In contrast, a physical optical lens is a curved piece of glass or plastic to refract light and focus it on a specific point. Lenses alter the way light passes through them and modify the formed image.

A metaphorical lens, similar to a physical lens, can change how we view and understand information. It can be shaped by various factors, such as cultural background or personal experiences, impacting how we interpret an idea.

The Y.E.A.R.N. Advantage provides a specific framework for analyzing and understanding the ideas behind the following values:

Y	YOU, the person.	SELF
E	Environment.	PLACES
A	Act.	TIME
R	Resources.	ENERGY
N	Networks. (relationships)	PEOPLE

The YEARN Advantage can help you gain clarity and perspective in different areas of your life. It provides a framework to filter your values through different categories and understand how they apply in various contexts.

Other ways to "see" through the lens of the YEARN Advantage include:

1. Using the YEARN Advantage to address personal and professional goals and aspirations and determine how they align with your beliefs and purpose.

2. Applying the YEARN Advantage to analyze and understand the motivations and behaviors of others and how they relate to your beliefs and purpose.

3. Leveraging the YEARN Advantage to identify and evaluate potential opportunities and determine if they align with your beliefs and purpose.

4. Practicing the YEARN Advantage to problem-solving and decision-making by filtering potential solutions and actions through your beliefs and purpose.

5. Employ the YEARN Advantage to evaluate and improve personal and professional relationships by understanding how they align with your beliefs and purpose and determining ways to strengthen them.

The set of five stories in the previous section, when viewed through the lens of the YEARN advantage, illustrates the importance of each of the five values.

Using the YEARN lens to consider and leverage each of the five values of the YEARN advantage can help you achieve your goals and improve your personal and professional life.

Here are some suggestions on how to stay true to your values:

1. You value yourself. You matter. YOU (self):

- Identify your personal values, passions, and goals, and pursue them with integrity and authenticity. If desired, create an enhavim: Your purpose and mission led by your vision.

- Take care of your physical, mental, emotional, and spiritual well-being. Engage in self-care practices that promote your health that are positive and uplifting.

- Practice self-reflection and self-awareness to understand your thoughts, emotions, and behaviors. Develop your virtues.

- Set boundaries that protect your time, energy, and emotional health.

- Stay true to yourself by being honest with yourself and others. Express your opinions and feelings respectfully, and stand up for what you believe in.

"Let me tell you the secret that has led me to my goal. My strength lies solely in my tenacity." - Louis Pasteur

2. You value your environments (online, offline):

- Foster a positive physical environment by keeping your surroundings clean, organized, and aesthetically pleasing.

- Be mindful of your impact on the environment by reducing waste, conserving resources, practicing sustainable living, and reducing your carbon footprint.

- Practice digital citizenship by being respectful, responsible, and ethical online. Avoid cyberbullying, respect others' privacy, and being mindful of the information you share online.

- Enjoy nature, choose supportive environments, and surround yourself with people who see your vision.

3. You act decisively for positive change (actions-time):

- Act with integrity and treat others with kindness, respect, and empathy. You value yourself and others.

- Set goals in your planning schedule that align with your values. Take steps towards achieving them, such as creating an enhavim with a big action plan.

- Take responsibility for the consequences of your actions and hold yourself accountable for mistakes or wrongdoing.

- Be proactive in identifying and addressing challenges and opportunities. Learn new skills or take on new responsibilities.

- Practice mindfulness in your actions. Be fully present and aware of your thoughts, emotions, and behaviors.

4. **To create results, you use, employ and develop valuable resources (tangible, intangible):**

- Build a diverse set of resources, such as financial, social, and intellectual capital. Network, volunteer, and seek out mentorship opportunities.

- Invest in your education, skills, and personal development by reading books, attending workshops, or taking courses.

- Be grateful for your resources and give back to others who may be less fortunate. Volunteer your time and skills, donate to charities, or support community projects and initiatives.

5. **You value your networks (people, relationships):**

- Build and maintain positive relationships with family, friends, and colleagues. Show appreciation, respect, and empathy toward them.

- Cultivate a diverse and supportive network that includes people from different backgrounds and perspectives. Seek opportunities to connect with others who share your values and interests.

- Practice active listening and empathy in your interactions with others by truly listening to what they have to say and considering their point of view.

- Be a good friend and ally by standing up for others. Provide emotional support or help as needed.

- Join a community organization dedicated to causes you wish to support. Advocate for social change. Work together with others towards a common goal, to create positive change and make a difference in your community and beyond.

Here is how we can collaborate:

Gather together.

Embrace God's Grace.

Love one another.

Live in Peace.

Advance Humanity.

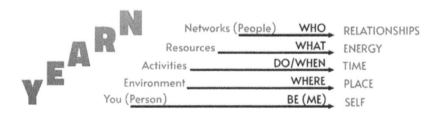

Figure 4 YEARN Core Stack

192

Did you notice that in Y.E.A.R.N., there is only one verb, and that verb is ACT?

Act is the value and the middle letter of the word, YEARN, and the top slice of the apple. Act ties all the values together.

When you act on your idea, you can make it a reality. This can bring progress, innovation, and development in the chosen field.

Take concrete steps such as creating a prototype, conducting market research, or launching a business. This can lead to job opportunities, economic growth, and a better quality of life. Similarly, taking intentional actions on a personal level can also result in self-growth and achievement of one's goals.

Acting on your idea can lead to positive outcomes. Failing to take action can result in missed opportunities and untapped potential.

What if JK Rowling had the idea for the *Harry Potter* story but never wrote it down; the world would have missed out on the value of that fantastic story!

Discussing verbs is more than an English grammar lesson. It is another way of seeing the five values of the YEARN advantage. It is about the actions to make progress on your road to greatness.

Action verbs and nouns are two distinct parts of speech that perform different functions in a sentence. An action verb is a word that conveys an action or a state of being, such as "run," "decide," "identify," or "exist." It describes an action that a subject can perform or a state that an issue can be in.

On the other hand, a noun is a word that represents a person, place, thing, or idea, such as "house," "people," or "love." Nouns can function as subjects, objects of a verb, or objects of a preposition. Sometimes, a noun can also be a verb, such as in the sentence, "I love you."

"Act" is a versatile verb that means to take action, perform a task or behave in a certain way. It can also mean to pretend or put on a performance, as in acting in a play or movie. "Act" is a verb that can be used in different tenses and forms, like "acted," "acting," or "will act," depending on the context and the time frame. In a sentence like "The man acted quickly during the house fire," "acted" is the action verb describing the man's quick action, while "man" is the subject of the sentence.

Verbs are closely linked to the passage of time because they indicate when an action or event occurs. Verbs can be used in different tenses, such as present, past, and future, to convey various aspects of time.

When you look at cycles in the next section, you will see how time and the YEARN advantage are connected.

Act means doing something over time, even for a few seconds. Action and time are intricately connected.

Verbs express action, convey meaning, indicate tense, and create sentence structure.

The verb "act" can be used in different tenses and forms to indicate when an action takes place or how long it lasts. For example, "I am taking action" is in the present progressive tense, "took action" is in the past tense, and "will take action" is in the future tense. Using different verb tenses helps create a timeline of events and provides details about when actions occurred, which is important in storytelling or recounting events. Some verbs can also indicate the duration of an action or event, such as "had been taking action."

Verbs play a crucial role in describing the passage of time and help to create a more detailed and nuanced understanding of events and actions. Nothing would happen without verbs, action words, and the actual "act" of doing.

Today is the time to decide and act,

Don't let indecision hold you back,

Act now to avoid future regret,

No deathbed remorse you'd rather forget.

The four nouns in the YEARN advantage:

1) **"YOU"** is a pronoun that refers to the person or people being addressed in a sentence. It is a second-person pronoun that relates to the person or people being spoken to or written to.

   In grammar, "you" can be a singular or plural pronoun. When addressing a single person, "you" is used as a singular pronoun. For example: "Can you pass me the salt, please?" When addressing multiple people, "you" is a plural pronoun. For example: "Are you all coming to the party tonight?"

   "You" is a ubiquitous word used in English in conversation and writing to address and refer to people. The term "you" is employed in crafty ways in advertising campaigns.

2) The noun **"ENVIRONMENT"** refers to the surroundings or conditions in which a person, animal, or plant lives or operates. Physical, built, social, digital, and cultural factors as well as natural and human-made elements impact and influence the existence and progress of the environment.

   Environment can refer to both the natural world and built, human-made surroundings, such as buildings, cities, and transportation systems. It includes interactions between living organisms and resources like air, water, and soil and ecosystems such as forests, oceans, and wildlife habitats. The term "environment" is a broad concept encompassing various physical, digital, and social aspects. It is often used in discussions of sustainability, climate change, and other environmental issues.

3) The noun **"RESOURCES"** refers to the available supplies or assets that can be used to achieve a particular goal or purpose. Depending on the context, it can refer to various things, such as natural, human, financial, or technological resources.

Resources are things found in nature or created by humans that are useful to achieve specific goals. Natural resources are materials like minerals, timber, and water that exist in nature. Human resources refer to people's skills, knowledge, and labor.

Financial resources refer to money and other assets used to invest, buy goods or services, or support economic activities. Technological resources refer to tools, machinery, and equipment that can produce goods or services or improve efficiency and productivity. Resources are the things that individuals, organizations, or societies can use to achieve their objectives. Resources are often used in economics, business, and resource management discussions.

4) The noun **"NETWORKS"** refers to a group or system of interconnected individuals or entities who communicate or work together to achieve a common goal. A network is a group of social, professional, or computer connections. In social or professional contexts, it describes a set of relationships based on shared interests, personal or professional affiliations, or other factors. A network can be a group of personal or business connections that share and achieve common goals.

#tyadvantage

Core Questions for YEARN

The following are questions for each of the five core values of the YEARN advantage. These questions will help spark your imagination.

Y: YOU

YOUR IDENTITY:

1. How have your history, upbringing, experiences, and relationships shaped your identity?

2. How do your personality traits, such as introversion or emotional stability, contribute to your identity?

3. How do your interests and hobbies contribute to your sense of self?

4. How has your family history, including ancestry and cultural heritage, influenced your self-perception and identity?

5. How has your culture and community shaped who you are?

6. How has the country or locale you are from influenced your identity?

7. How has your race and ethnicity influenced your cultural background, experiences, and perspectives?

8. How has your gender and sexuality impacted how you see yourself and how others perceive you?

9. How has your physical and mental health influenced your identity and interactions with others?

10. How has your religion or spirituality shaped your beliefs, values, and behaviors?

11. How have your relationships with others, such as family, friends, and romantic partners, influenced your self-perception and identity?

YOUR BELIEFS AND VALUES:

12. How have your formal education and informal learning experiences influenced your beliefs and perspectives?

13. How have your religious beliefs shaped your worldview, attitudes, and behaviors? How do you pursue inner peace through spiritual practices?

14. How has the media you consume shaped your beliefs and opinions on different topics and issues?

15. How have significant life experiences, such as personal successes or failures, traumatic experiences, or major life transitions, shaped your beliefs?

16. How do societal expectations around gender impact beliefs and perspectives?

17. How have your peer groups and social networks influenced your attitudes and opinions?

18. How has your racial and ethnic identity influenced your beliefs and values?

19. How has your location and the regional, national, or global context in which you live influenced your beliefs and perspectives?

20. How have language and the cultural meanings associated with different languages influenced your beliefs?

21. How have personality traits, such as openness to experience, neuroticism, or agreeableness, influenced your beliefs and perspectives?

22. How have traumatic experiences, such as war, abuse, violence, or loss, shaped your beliefs and perspectives?

23. How has historical context, such as significant events and trends, shaped your beliefs and political affiliations?

24. How does social class or economic status impact your beliefs and values within your culture?

YOUR INFLUENCES:

25. How has access to resources and money, such as socioeconomic status or education, molded your identity?

26. How has technology influenced your beliefs and experiences in the world?

27. How does social class or economic status impact beliefs and values within a culture?

28. How have your experiences with different cultures and lifestyles influenced your beliefs and values?

29. How has your exposure to different forms of art and media shaped your perspectives and understanding of the world?

30. How do your political beliefs and affiliations inform your values and worldview?

31. How has your occupation or career path influenced your identity and beliefs?

32. How do societal norms and expectations influence your sense of self and values?

YOUR DEVELOPMENT AND SELF-IMPROVEMENT

33. Identify Your Goals: What steps can you take to ensure that you set realistic goals for yourself, and what strategies can you use to achieve them?

34. Vision and Purpose: How can establishing a clear vision and purpose help you make better decisions and take more purposeful actions toward self-improvement?

35. Focus on Your Strengths: How can you identify your unique strengths, and how can you work on honing those skills to increase your confidence and resilience?

36. Address Your Weaknesses: How can you acknowledge your areas of weakness and turn them into opportunities for growth and improvement?

37. Proactivity and Control: What steps can you take to take the initiative and take control of your own life instead of letting life control you?

38. Focus on what matters: How can you prioritize what matters most in your life, such as relationships, values, and goals, to stay focused and on track?

39. Be willing to be seen as imperfect: How can you accept and embrace your faults and mistakes as essential to self-improvement and use criticism as a learning opportunity?

40. Be Joyful: How can you find joy in the little things and cultivate gratitude for the blessings in your life, leading to a more fulfilling life?

41. Learn, Learn, & Learn: How can you incorporate lifelong learning into your life, whether through formal education, online courses, or self-study, to continue to grow and develop as an individual?

42. Learn to Confront and Initiate Change: How can you step out of your comfort zone and initiate change, even when it feels intimidating or scary, to grow and expand your horizons?

43. Live in the Now: How can you learn to be more present, embrace risk-taking, and seize opportunities as they come your way?

44. Personal Self-Care: What effective self-care practices can you incorporate into your life, such as mindfulness and exercise, to show self-love and improve your overall well-being?

45. Create your legacy daily: How can you start building a positive reputation and legacy for yourself, and why is it essential to do so in today's world?

You have GREATNESS in you!
~Les Brown

E: ENVIRONMENT

BUILT ENVIRONMENT:

1. How can you make your home or office space more conducive to productivity and well-being?

2. How can you advocate for and contribute to developing sustainable and environmentally friendly urban spaces in your community?

3. What strategies can you use to create more inclusive and accessible public spaces that meet the needs of diverse individuals and communities?

PHYSICAL and NATURAL ENVIRONMENT:

4. What can you do to reduce your carbon footprint and contribute to the preservation of our natural resources?

5. How can you stay informed about environmental issues and advocate for policies and actions that protect our planet?

6. What steps can you take to cultivate a greater sense of wonder and appreciation for the natural world, even in your everyday life?

7. Where can you go to experience more of nature regularly?

8. How can you make your living and working spaces more environmentally friendly by using energy-efficient appliances and reducing waste?

9. How can you support local agriculture and sustainable food practices, such as buying from farmers' markets or starting a fruit or vegetable garden?

10. How can you participate in conservation efforts to protect endangered species and their habitats?

11. How can you incorporate outdoor activities and exercise into your routine while also enjoying and connecting with nature?

12. How can you encourage others to take actions that benefit the environment, such as by starting a community recycling program or organizing a beach clean-up event?

DIGITAL ENVIRONMENT:

13. How can you use digital technologies to enhance your personal and professional goals while being mindful of potential adverse effects such as addiction and online harassment?

14. What strategies can you use to protect your personal information and privacy online while taking advantage of digital communication and commerce?

15. What role can you play in promoting a more equitable and ethical digital environment by advocating for fair labor practices and responsible data management?

16. How can you improve your online presence and build a solid personal brand using digital tools and platforms?

17. How can you use social media to build and maintain professional relationships and expand your network?

18. What practical ways can digital tools and resources be used for remote work and collaboration?

19. How can you develop digital literacy skills and stay up-to-date with the latest technologies and trends?

20. How can you use digital resources to access educational opportunities and advance your career goals, such as online courses and training programs?

21. What are some potential risks and benefits of using artificial intelligence in various aspects of your personal and professional life, and how can you make informed decisions about its use?

CULTURAL ENVIRONMENT:

22. How can you engage with diverse cultural perspectives and experiences, such as by exploring different genres of music or reading works by authors from different backgrounds?

23. What role can you play in promoting greater cultural understanding and respect in your community, such as by participating in interfaith dialogues or supporting local arts organizations?

24. How can you cultivate a personal sense of meaning and purpose through your engagement with culture and community, such as by participating in volunteer work or attending cultural events?

ECONOMIC ENVIRONMENT:

25. How can you educate yourself about economic issues and policies that affect your personal finances and the broader society?

26. What steps can you take to promote economic justice and reduce inequality in your community and beyond?

27. How can you balance your personal goals and values with the pressures of the more extensive economic system, such as by pursuing socially responsible investments and career paths?

A: ACT

YOUR ACTIONS

ACTION IN WORK & PRODUCTIVITY:

1. How can you set and maintain high standards in your work and productivity to achieve success?

2. What strategies can you use to persist and overcome obstacles in your pursuit of greatness?

3. How can you prioritize your tasks and manage your time efficiently to maximize productivity?

4. How can you stay motivated and focused on your goals in the face of challenges and setbacks?

5. How can you balance the need for quality work with the need for efficiency and speed?

6. What effective communication techniques can you use to work collaboratively with others and achieve common goals?

7. How can you develop and cultivate leadership skills to inspire and motivate others in your workplace or industry?

8. What role does creativity play in work and productivity, and how can you cultivate a creative mindset to improve your career?

9. How can you foster a positive work environment encouraging productivity and teamwork?

10. How can you continually incorporate feedback from others to improve your work and achieve better results?

ACTIONS & YOUR TYPE

11. How can you identify whether you tend to approach action-taking as an idealist, cynic, or realist?

12. As an idealist, what steps can you take to stay motivated toward achieving long-term goals, despite setbacks or challenges?

13. If you tend to be a cynic, what strategies can you use to overcome skepticism and develop a more optimistic outlook while still being realistic?

14. How can you balance short-term and long-term thinking, especially if you tend to be a realist, to ensure that you are progressing towards your goals while still being pragmatic?

15. How can you leverage your action-taking to work with others with different perspectives, such as idealists, cynics, or realists, to achieve collective success?

ACTION & ADAPTABILITY:

16. When do you know when to change your actions? How can you adapt to changing circumstances and be open to new experiences?

17. What are some signs that it may be time to change your actions or approach to a particular situation?

18. How can you cultivate a growth mindset and embrace challenges as opportunities for learning and growth?

19. What strategies can you use to overcome resistance to change and take action toward adapting to new circumstances?

20. How can you stay focused on your goals and values while remaining flexible and adaptable in your approach?

TIME & PRIORITIZING ACTIONS:

21. How can you prioritize your actions to align with your values and goals?

22. Have you ever felt like you didn't have enough time to take the actions you wanted to take? How did you handle it?

23. How do you balance taking actions that are important for your long-term goals with taking actions that are necessary for your immediate needs?

24. Have you ever had to change your priorities or actions because of a change in circumstances? How did you adapt?

25. In what ways does your perception of time affect the actions you take?

26. What strategies can you use to manage your time more effectively and increase productivity?

27. How can you avoid procrastination and stay motivated to take action towards your goals?

28. What role can delegation and outsourcing play in helping you prioritize your actions and manage your time more efficiently?

29. How can you make the most of small pockets of time throughout your day to make progress towards your goals?

30. How can you determine which actions are most important and will significantly impact achieving your goals?

31. How can you balance the need to take action with the importance of rest and self-care to avoid burnout and maintain long-term productivity?

SHORT-TERM, LONG-TERM ACTIONS & HABITS:

32. What short-term professional actions can you take to enhance your skills in your current job?

33. What short-term professional actions can you take to improve your resume and make yourself more attractive to potential employers?

34. What long-term personal actions can you take to improve your health and well-being?

35. What long-term professional actions can you take to advance your career to the next level?

36. What short-term personal habits can you develop to reduce stress and improve your daily routine?

37. What long-term personal habits can you develop to improve your financial stability and save for the future?

38. What short-term professional habits can you develop to increase your productivity and efficiency at work?

39. What long-term professional habits can you develop to become a more effective leader and mentor to your colleagues?

LIVELIHOOD, TALENT, & LEARNING ACTIONS:

40. What are some intelligent actions you can take to improve your job performance and increase your chances of career advancement?

41. What steps can you take to start and grow your own business, even if you don't have a background in entrepreneurship?

42. How can you ensure a steady livelihood for yourself and your family, even during economic uncertainty?

43. What are some examples of talent-skill development actions you can take to improve your abilities in your chosen field?

44. How can you effectively learn to play a musical instrument without prior experience or training?

45. What are some practical ways to improve your writing skills and produce more compelling and persuasive content?

46. How can you master a new language and communicate more effectively with people from different cultures?

47. How can you develop your artistic skills and bring your creative ideas to life, even if you're not a professional artist?

48. What are some effective ways to learn how to code, even if you have no prior experience in programming?

49. What are some examples of learning actions you can take to improve your critical thinking skills and make better decisions in your personal and professional life?

HOBBIES, LEGACY, CHARITY & CAUSES ACTIONS:

50. Where are the hiking trails that you can explore in your local area, and how can you ensure that you're adequately prepared for each hike?

51. How can you improve your photography skills and take better pictures, whether you're using a professional camera or just your smartphone?

52. What outstanding books can you read to relax and unwind, and how can you find time to read more often?

53. What are some tips for getting started with painting, even if you have no prior experience or artistic training?

54. What exciting travel destinations can you visit, and how can you plan your itinerary effectively to make the most of your trip?

55. What steps can you take to start building a legacy that will outlive you while you're still alive?

56. How can you ensure that your values and beliefs are reflected in the legacy you leave behind, and whom do you admire who has successfully done this?

57. What are the family traditions and stories you want to pass down through the generations?

58. What are effective ways to research and choose a charity to donate to?

59. What creative ways to raise funds for a charity, and how can you involve your network in your fundraising efforts?

60. How can you make a lasting impact through volunteer work, and what non-paid opportunities allow you to make a meaningful difference in your community?

61. What social justice issues are worth advocating for, and how can you use your voice and platform to raise awareness and effect change?

62. What environmental causes are worth supporting, and how can you make a difference in reducing your carbon footprint?

63. How can you support important causes even if you don't have much money or resources to donate, and what are some creative ways to get involved in these causes?

R: RESOURCES

PERSONAL FINANCE & WEALTH MANAGEMENT RESOURCES:

1. How can you utilize your available resources to make more informed financial choices?

2. How can you balance your financial resources to achieve both short-term and long-term goals?

3. In what ways can an individual borrow resources to help them achieve their objectives?

4. How can someone negotiate to obtain the necessary resources to achieve their goals?

5. What are some risks associated with leveraging resources to achieve objectives?

6. What financial strategies can you implement to make the most out of your available resources?

7. How can you leverage your personal talents and skills to improve your financial situation?

8. How can networking and human connections help you acquire new resources and improve your financial prospects?

9. What educational opportunities can you take advantage of to increase your financial literacy and make better financial choices?

10. How can you stay resourceful and adaptable in changing financial circumstances?

11. How can you track your spending and analyze your financial habits to make more informed financial choices?

12. How can you prioritize your financial goals and allocate your resources accordingly?

13. What are effective ways to save and invest your money to achieve long-term financial security?

14. How can you negotiate better deals and prices to maximize your financial resources?

15. How can you build and maintain a strong credit score to access more financial opportunities?

16. What role do financial advisors or planners play in helping you make informed financial choices, and how can you find the right one for you?

17. How can you manage debt and financial obligations while achieving your goals?

18. How can you use technology and online resources to manage your finances more efficiently and effectively?

19. What are some ethical considerations when making financial choices and using your resources?

20. How can you evaluate and compare financial products and services to best meet your needs and goals?

21. Can a lack of resources ever be an advantage? If so, how?

ENTREPRENEURSHIP & BUSINESS RESOURCES:

22. How can you stay resourceful and adaptable in changing financial circumstances?

23. What bootstrapping strategies can you use to launch and grow your business with limited resources?

24. How can you identify and secure funding opportunities, such as grants, crowdfunding, and angel investors, to finance your business venture?

25. What are the benefits and drawbacks of different financing options, such as bank loans and venture capital, and how can you determine the best fit for your business?

26. How can you evaluate and compare financial products and services to best meet your business needs and goals?

INTANGIBLE RESOURCES:

27. What intangible resources can you draw upon to navigate difficult situations in your life?

28. How can you develop emotional intelligence to improve interpersonal relationships?

29. How might someone leverage their reputation to achieve their objectives?

30. What intangible resources can you utilize to cultivate a sense of purpose and meaning in your life?

31. How can you leverage your creativity and imagination to solve problems and develop new ideas?

32. How do intangible resources differ from tangible ones regarding their value?

33. Can intangible resources be more valuable than tangible ones? Why or why not?

EDUCATIONAL RESOURCES:

34. What educational resources can you access to learn a new skill or trade?

35. How can you use online educational resources to further your career?

36. What educational resources are available to help you improve your financial literacy?

37. How can you leverage mentorship and apprenticeship programs to gain hands-on experience in your field?

38. What educational resources can you use to improve your communication and collaboration skills?

GENERATIONAL RESOURCES:

39. How can you learn from the wisdom and experience of previous generations?

40. What generational resources can you access to understand the cultural and historical context of your community?

41. How can you connect with and learn from people of different age groups and backgrounds?

42. What generational resources can you use to preserve and pass on cultural traditions and practices?

43. How can you leverage intergenerational relationships to foster mutual understanding and respect?

COMMUNITY RESOURCES:

44. What community resources can you access to support your physical and mental health?

45. How can you use local community centers and programs to build social connections?

46. What community resources can you rely on to promote environmental sustainability?

47. How can you utilize community resources to address social and economic inequalities?

48. What community resources are available to help you start or grow a small business?

N: NETWORK

INTERPERSONAL RELATIONSHIPS:

1. How can you build healthy, positive relationships with those around you?

2. What practical ways can you communicate your needs and boundaries in relationships?

3. How can you navigate conflicts and disagreements constructively and respectfully?

4. How do you build trust and deepen connections with others over time?

5. How can you show appreciation and gratitude for the people in your life who support and inspire you?

COLLABORATION & INNOVATION:

6. How can you foster an environment encouraging innovation and creativity within your relationships and networks?

7. What are some strategies for collaborating effectively with others, whether in a personal or professional context?

8. How can you leverage the diverse perspectives and strengths of those around you to achieve shared goals?

9. What are some ways to approach problem-solving and decision-making collaboratively rather than individually?

10. How can you stay open-minded and receptive to new ideas and perspectives, even when they challenge your assumptions?

KINDNESS:

11. How can you cultivate a spirit of kindness and generosity in your interactions with others?

12. What are some small acts of kindness that can have a significant impact on the people around you?

13. How can you practice empathy and understanding in your relationships, even when you may disagree with someone else's perspective?

14. How can you show compassion and support to those who are going through difficult times?

15. How can you model kindness and encourage others to do the same?

AN ABILITY TO CONNECT:

1. How can you improve your ability to connect with others more deeply?

2. What practical ways to build rapport and establish trust with new people?

3. How can you develop your emotional intelligence to better understand and empathize with those around you?

4. What are some ways to actively listen and create a safe space for others to share their thoughts and feelings?

5. How can you foster an environment of vulnerability and authenticity in your relationships?

LOVING:

6. How can you cultivate love and compassion for yourself, as well as for others?

7. How do you express love and affection to the essential people in your life?

8. How can you create a sense of intimacy and connection in your romantic relationships?

9. How can you navigate the challenges and complexities of love, such as jealousy and conflict?

10. What are some ways to show love and support to those in your life who may be struggling or going through a difficult time?

LEAVING A LEGACY:

11. How can you live a life that aligns with your values and positively impacts the world?

12. How do you identify and pursue your mission or purpose?

13. How can you leave a legacy beyond your lifetime by mentoring and supporting future generations?

14. How do you measure your impact and assess whether you are achieving your goals for leaving a legacy?

15. How can you celebrate and honor the legacies of those who came before you while also forging your own path?

PART
IV

Delving Deeper into YEARN

APPLES are known as the almost perfect food. Most apples have five seed pockets or carpels, and this follows the five core values of the YEARN Advantage.

Other systems and books identify *desires* (related to yearning), and these frameworks are not mutually exclusive. There may be overlaps or differences in defining and categorizing people's core desires or values.

"God gave us the gift of life; it is up to us to
give ourselves the gift of living well."
~Voltaire

Your desire and motivation are tied to your expectations. Expectations don't necessarily define your performance, but having high standards can help you achieve greatness.

Compare The YEARN Advantage to the Wheel of Life

The YEARN Advantage and the Wheel of Life are excellent resources to take stock of and upgrade your life. Y.E.A.R.N. stands for You, Environment, Act, Resources, and Network and encourages you to master the five core values in your life. It's visualized as an apple cut into five slices, each symbolizing one of the five values.

In contrast, the Wheel of Life is a customizable graph of different aspects of your life, allowing you to include any number of areas. It's used to check your life balance and pinpoint areas that need more attention. Its primary purpose is to evaluate and reflect.

Although the YEARN Advantage and the Wheel of Life share similarities, there are also differences. The YEARN Advantage is a specific mnemonic that focuses on the five core values and encourages you to take action to reach greatness.

The YEARN advantage and the Wheel of Life can help you identify areas that need improvement. YEARN's value of 'Act' encourages you to take steps to achieve your ambitions and realize your potential.

The Wheel of Life provides a snapshot of your current life, allowing you to take stock of where you are. On the other hand, the YEARN advantage focuses on what you can achieve in the future. It emphasizes the need for action and encourages you to use the five core values to achieve greatness.

DESIRES, ASPIRATIONS, MOTIVATIONS

Here is a compiled list of motivations that most people can relate to:

1. *Autonomy:* the desire to control one's life and decisions and to have freedom and independence. (Personal Agency)

2. *Belongingness*: the desire to feel a sense of connection and acceptance with others, to be part of a group or community, and to have meaningful relationships.

3. *Competence*: the desire to feel capable and effective at tasks and challenges and to develop skills and mastery in areas of interest.

4. *Self-expression*: the desire to express oneself authentically and creatively.

5. *Spirituality*: the desire to seek meaning and purpose beyond material possessions and external achievements. Transcendence and connection with a higher power or spiritual reality.

6. *Altruism:* the desire to help others and positively impact the world.

7. *Hedonism:* the desire for pleasure and sensory gratification.

8. *Curiosity:* the desire for knowledge, exploration, and new experiences, to understand the world and how it works, and to learn and develop.

9. *Justice:* the desire for fairness, equality, and social justice.

10. *Order:* the desire for structure, organization, and predictability in one's environment to establish routine and stability in one's life.

11. *Recognition*: the desire to be acknowledged, appreciated, and recognized for one's efforts, accomplishments, or contributions.

12. *Power:* the desire to control or influence others, to achieve authority or dominance, or to feel powerful and vital.

13. *Safety:* the desire for physical and emotional security to feel protected and safe from harm, danger, or threats.

14. *Creativity*: the desire to express oneself creatively, to be innovative, and to produce something new or unique.

15. *Beauty:* the desire for aesthetic pleasure, to appreciate and experience beauty in art, nature, music, and other forms of expression.

16. *Freedom:* the desire for autonomy, independence, and self-determination, to have the power to make choices and act on them.

17. *Growth*: the desire to learn and develop, to explore new experiences and ideas, and to expand one's understanding of the world.

18. *Purpose*: the desire to have a sense of meaning and direction in life, to pursue goals that align with one's values and beliefs, and to make a positive contribution to society.

Napoleon Hill was an American self-help author best known for his book *"Think and Grow Rich."* He believed the 12 desires he wrote about were essential to leading a successful and fulfilling life. Apart from the missing E, environment, each of Hill's 12 desires can be categorized by the YEARN core values.

YOU

1. *Sound physical health:* the desire to maintain a healthy and fit body and to take care of one's physical well-being.

2. *Positive mental attitude*: the desire to maintain an optimistic and constructive mindset and focus on life's positive aspects.

3. *An open mind on all subjects:* the desire to be curious and receptive to new ideas and perspectives and to be willing to consider different viewpoints and opinions.

4. *The capacity for applied faith*: the desire to have a robust belief system and to apply one's faith in practical ways to overcome challenges and achieve success.

5. *Freedom from fear:* the desire to overcome fear and anxiety and to live a life free from worry and stress.

6. *The Hope of Future Achievements:* the desire to have a sense of purpose and direction and to strive towards achieving personal and professional goals. (Something to look forward to)

ACT

7. *To be engaged in a labor of love:* the desire to pursue work or activities that are personally fulfilling and meaningful and to find joy and satisfaction in one's endeavors. Labor of Love, Livelihood. Grand Plan, Hobbies. (Something to do and look forward to)

8. *Self-discipline:* the desire to control one's behavior and habits and stick to commitments and goals.

- Habit Motivation: The driving force compels you to perform the habit. Stronger the motivation, the more you're engaged.
- Habit Trigger: An event or signal that initiates the habit. It could be a specific time of day, a location, an emotion, a person, or a cue that prompts you to perform the habit.
- Habit Behavior: The action or response you take in reaction to the trigger and motivation. It's the habit itself.
- Habit Reinforcement: A positive outcome or benefit you receive from performing the habit. The stronger the reinforcement, the more likely you will perform it again.

RESOURCES

9. *Economic security*: the desire to have financial stability and security and to provide for oneself and one's family.

NETWORK

10. *Harmony in human relationships:* the desire to maintain peaceful and positive relationships in various networks and to avoid conflicts and misunderstandings. (Someone to love)

11. *Willingness to share one's blessings with others*: the desire to be generous and compassionate towards others and to share one's resources and benefits to help those in need.

12. *The capacity to understand people*: the desire to have empathy and compassion towards others and to understand and relate to their thoughts and feelings.

Cycles

YEAR

YEAR – the first four letters of "YEARN."

Year Etymology

year (n.)

The word "year" is a fascinating term with a rich history and cultural significance. Let's delve into its etymology, the concept of time it represents, and how it has been used throughout human history.

The word "year" derives from the Old English "gear" or "geār," which originally referred to a complete cycle of seasons, from spring to winter. Gears are a component of cycling, as in a bicycle.

The word year itself can be traced back to the Proto-Germanic word "jǣran," which has the same root as the Latin word "annulus," meaning "year." The concept of the year has been an integral part of human culture and history, with various civilizations developing their systems of measuring time which is based on the cycle of seasons and celestial movements.

Concept of Time:

Time is part of Core Value #3, ACT. A year is commonly defined as the time it takes for the Earth to complete one orbit around the Sun. This period is approximately 365.25 days, which is why we have a leap year every four years to adjust for this slight discrepancy. The concept of a year varies depending on cultural and religious beliefs. For example, the Islamic calendar is based on the lunar cycle and consists of 12 lunar months, meaning a year in the Islamic calendar is 11 days shorter than a solar year.

The concept of a year is deeply ingrained in our understanding of time and how we measure our lives. It provides us with a sense of continuity and allows us to track the passage of time, marking important events and milestones along the way. For many people, the start of a new year is a time for reflection, goal-setting, and fresh beginnings.

History and Culture:

The concept of a year has been used throughout human history in various ways, from agricultural cycles to religious calendars. The ancient Egyptians, for example, used a calendar based on the annual flooding of the Nile River, which marked the start of their agricultural cycle. On the other hand, the Mayans had a complex calendar system that included multiple cycles of days, months, and years, which they used to track astronomical events and religious festivals.

In modern times, the year concept has taken on new cultural significance. New Year's Eve, celebrated on December 31st, is a time of revelry and reflection in many cultures worldwide. It's the end of one year and the beginning of the next, and is often accompanied by fireworks, parties, and resolutions for the year ahead.

The word "year" is a fundamental concept in our understanding of time and how we measure the passage of our lives. Its etymology can be traced back to ancient roots, and its cultural significance has evolved throughout human history. Whether we mark the passing of time through the cycle of seasons, the movement of celestial bodies, or the milestones of our lives, the year is a unit of time deeply ingrained in our collective consciousness.

Cycle of Seasons

The cycle of seasons is a fundamental aspect of the concept of a year and has been a critical factor in measuring time and marking important events throughout human history.

The cycle of seasons is caused by the Earth's axial tilt, which causes different regions of the planet to receive varying amounts of sunlight throughout the year. In the Northern Hemisphere, for example, the summer solstice occurs around June 21st, marking the longest day of the year and the start of summer. The winter solstice occurs around December 21st, marking the year's shortest day and the beginning of winter. Various cultures have used these astronomical events throughout history to mark vital times of the year, such as religious festivals, agricultural cycles, and hunting seasons.

The cycle of seasons has also significantly impacted human culture and society. For example, the agricultural revolution, which began around 10,000 years ago, was made possible by the ability of humans to cultivate crops and domesticate animals. This was mainly due to the development of agricultural calendars based on the cycle of seasons, allowing farmers to plant and harvest crops at the appropriate times.

In many cultures, the cycle of seasons is deeply intertwined with religious beliefs and practices. For example, the Christian holiday of Easter is celebrated in the spring, marking the resurrection of Jesus and symbolizing new beginnings and rebirth. The Hindu festival of Holi, also known as the "Festival of Colors," is celebrated in the spring to mark the end of winter and the start of the harvest season.

The cycle of seasons is a fundamental aspect of the concept of a year and has played a significant role in human culture and society throughout history. Whether marking the passage of time through religious festivals, agricultural cycles, or personal milestones, the changing of the seasons continues to be a powerful symbol of renewal, growth, and change.

What are the major CULTURAL annual events that occur over a year?

Many major annual events with significance and cultural traditions occur over a year. Here are some examples of major annual events in *Western* culture (there are many more worldwide):

New Year's Day: Celebrated on January 1st, this is a time to reflect on the past year and make resolutions for the coming year. It is a time for fresh starts and new beginnings. (Did you know that in the 16th century, there was a switch from the Julian to the Gregorian calendar, moving New Year's Day from April 1st to January 1st? This supports the idea that time is perceived as a cultural and cognitive construct.)

Valentine's Day: Celebrated February 14th is a day to celebrate love and affection. It is often marked by exchanging cards, flowers, and gifts between romantic partners.

St. Patrick's Day: Celebrated on March 17th is a day to celebrate Irish culture and heritage. It is often marked by parades, wearing green, and drinking Guinness.

Easter: Celebrated in the spring, this is a major Christian holiday commemorating Jesus Christ. She is celebrated with church services, Easter egg hunts, and the exchange of Easter baskets.

Mother's Day and Father's Day: Celebrated on separate days in May and June, these holidays honor parents and parental figures.

Independence Day: Celebrated on July 4th in the United States, this holiday commemorates the country's declaration of independence from Great Britain in 1776. They are celebrated with parades, barbecues, and fireworks.

Halloween: Celebrated on October 31st, this is a day to celebrate all things spookily and supernatural. It boasts costume parties, trick-or-treating, and pumpkin carving.

Thanksgiving: Celebrated on the fourth Thursday in November in the United States, this holiday is dedicated to giving thanks and showing appreciation for the blessings in life. It features a large family meal featuring turkey, stuffing, and pumpkin pie.

Christmas: Celebrated on December 25th, this is a major Christian holiday commemorating Jesus Christ's birth—a holiday known for gift-giving, Christmas carols, and decorating Christmas trees.

There are other major annual events, and one has its cultural significance and traditions and provides an opportunity to celebrate and commemorate important moments in life.

What are the major PERSONAL annual events that occur over a year?

Many major personal annual events occur over a year, each with its significant traditions. Here are some examples of major individual yearly events:

Birthday: This annual celebration of one's birth is typically marked by parties, gifts, and well-wishes from family and friends.

Anniversary: This is an annual celebration of the date of a significant event, such as a wedding or the start of a relationship. Special outings or gifts between partners often mark it.

Graduation: This is an annual event for students who complete a degree program and is often marked by a ceremony and celebration with family and friends.

Career Milestones: These annual events mark progress and achievements, such as annual performance reviews, promotions, and work anniversaries.

Health Check-Ups: These annual events involve visiting a doctor or health care professional to assess one's health and well-being. Examples include annual physical exams, dental check-ups, and vision exams.

Religious Holidays: Depending on one's religious affiliation, there may be annual events that are significant and filled with traditions and celebrations, such as Lent, Eid al-Fitr, or Hanukkah.

Vacation Time: An annual vacation is an important personal event that allows one to recharge, relax, and explore new places and experiences.

Personal Milestones: These annual events mark accomplishments or milestones, such as reaching a fitness goal, completing a personal project, or taking up a new hobby.

These are just a few annual personal events that occur over a year. Each provides an opportunity to reflect, celebrate, and acknowledge significant moments in one's life.

What are the significant Business occurrences or events that occur over a year?

Many major business occurrences and events occur over a year, each with significance and impact on a company's success. Here are some examples of significant business events:

Annual Budgeting and Planning: This is a yearly event where businesses plan their budgets and set goals for the upcoming year. It is typically a time to review past performance, identify improvement areas, and set growth targets.

Quarterly Earnings Reports: Publicly traded companies must report their financial performance every quarter, which can impact their stock prices and reputation.

Industry Conferences and Trade Shows: These events allow businesses to showcase their products and services, network with industry professionals, and follow the latest trends and developments.

Product Launches: Businesses may choose to launch new products or services throughout the year, which can involve extensive planning, marketing, and promotional activities.

Annual Performance Reviews: Many businesses conduct yearly performance reviews for employees, including setting goals, providing feedback, and discussing compensation.

Investor Relations: Publicly traded companies must maintain relationships with their investors, which may involve annual meetings, investor calls, and regular communication about the company's performance and direction.

Employee Recognition and Celebrations: Many businesses recognize and celebrate employee milestones, such as work anniversaries or reaching sales goals, to boost morale and promote positive company culture.

Cybersecurity Planning and Training: Cybersecurity threats are an ongoing concern for businesses, and annual planning and training can help mitigate risks and protect against potential breaches.

These are a few examples of major business occurrences and events over a year. Each one requires careful planning, preparation, and execution to achieve success and meet business objectives.

Here are some additional examples of significant business occurrences and events that occur over the course of a year:

Annual Corporate Retreat: Many businesses hold a yearly retreat for employees, which can involve team-building activities, strategic planning sessions, and opportunities for networking and relationship-building.

Tax Season: Businesses must file their taxes quarterly and annually, a complex process requiring careful planning and compliance with legal regulations.

Board of Directors Meetings: Publicly traded companies typically hold regular meetings of their board of directors, which can involve reviewing financial performance, setting company direction, and discussing shareholder concerns.

Employee Benefits Enrollment: Many businesses offer benefits such as health insurance and retirement plans, which require annual enrollment periods and ongoing management.

End-of-Year Inventory and Sales: Many businesses conduct end-of-year inventory checks and offer special sales or promotions to boost year-end revenue and clear out inventory.

Each event requires careful planning, preparation, and execution to succeed and meet business objectives. By effectively managing these events, businesses can build stronger relationships with employees, investors, and customers and ultimately position themselves for long-term success.

REVIEW Question for 'BUSINESS'

1. What do you want YOUR business life to look like?

2. What annual revenue would you like to generate?

3. What type of work do you want to do (products, services)?

4. What type of culture do you want to create?

5. To whom will we deliver the above services?

Effort

EARN

EARN – the last four letters of "YEARN."

Earn Etymology

earn (v.)

To earn something means to put in the effort. Old English *earnian* "deserve, earn, merit, labor for, win, get a reward for labor," from Proto-Germanic **aznon* "do harvest work, serve."

The word "earn" is a verb that describes the act of acquiring something through hard work, effort, or skill. The term earn is associated with earning money or financial compensation for work done. It can also be applied to other areas, such as earning respect or recognition.

The etymology of the word "earn" can be traced back to Old English, where it was spelled "earnian" and meant to reap or harvest. This sense of harvesting can be seen as a metaphor for the act of earning, where one puts in effort and work and receives a reward or benefit as a result. The harvest is a cycle, and the earning received at completion or "harvest time."

In Greek, the word *axía* means worthiness, value, merit, valuation, and deserving. The original Greek word for honor means worth or value but in a very literal sense. Honor was a culturally constructed evaluation of a person's actions, which determined a person's worth, as in their price or value to the community.

In modern usage, earning is most commonly associated with financial compensation for work done. Earning money can be earned by an employer's salary or hourly wage or by earning income from freelance or entrepreneurial work. To earn money, one must usually provide value to others by offering a product or service or working for a larger organization or company.

"Earning capacity" is "income potential." Income potential is the maximum amount of money an individual or business can earn based on their skills, education, experience, and other factors, assuming they operate optimally.

Known for his financial acumen, each topic that follows includes a quote from Warren Buffet.

Build value worth sharing.

"Price is what you pay. Value is what you get." ~Warren Buffett

Legacy is longevity.

"Investing should be more like watching paint dry or watching grass grow. If you want excitement, take $800 and go to Las Vegas." ~Warren Buffett

Act long-term.

"The stock market is a device for transferring money from the impatient to the patient." "The most important quality for an investor is temperament, not intellect." ~Warren Buffett

Take a proactive pause.

"I never attempt to make money on the stock market. I buy assuming they could close the market the next day and not reopen it for five years." ~Warren Buffett

Can you bounce back?

"Risk comes from not knowing what you're doing." "The biggest investment risk is not the volatility of prices, but whether you will suffer a permanent loss of capital." ~Warren Buffett

Earning is a concept that is tied to the idea of work and effort. Whether earning money or respect, the process often involves putting in time, energy, and skill and receiving a reward or benefit.

What is "earn the right"?

"Earn the right" is a phrase that is often used in the context of earning respect or gaining a particular privilege. It means to be deserving of something. The concept reminds us to take ownership of our actions and put in the necessary effort to achieve our goals and earn respect from others.

Earning can be applied to other areas of life, such as 'earning respect' or recognition. To earn respect, one must demonstrate valued qualities or skills like integrity, reliability, or creativity and build strong relationships with others. This can be achieved by listening well, showing empathy and understanding.

"Earning the right" is based on the idea that nothing worth having comes easily or without effort. It is a reminder that success, respect, and privileges must be earned through work and dedication rather than being handed out freely.

"Earning the right" is about taking personal responsibility, being accountable, and persevering towards achieving goals to gain respect and privileges from others. This concept requires individuals to prove themselves and put in the necessary effort and work to achieve their desired outcome. The idea is that we can only expect to be given things by first demonstrating our worthiness.

In a professional context, "earning the right" might mean proving yourself through effort and consistently meeting expectations before being given a promotion or higher-level responsibilities. It involves demonstrating your ability to handle the new role's responsibilities, showing initiative and leadership skills, and being committed to the company's values and direction. More than simply having tenure or a certain degree is required to be promoted.

In a personal context, "earning the right" might mean building a strong relationship with someone based on trust, integrity, and loyalty. You have to demonstrate these qualities to earn someone's respect and trust. Simply asking for it is not enough.

Understanding

EAR

EAR – the middle three letters of "YEARN."

Ear Etymology

ear (n.)

The word "ear" has a rich history and meaning in terms of its etymology and its role in human perception and communication.

Etymologically, the word "ear" can be traced back to the Old English word "*ēare*," which is also related to the Old Norse "*eyra*." This suggests a common ancestor in the Proto-Germanic language, which likely originated more than 2,000 years ago. Over time, the word evolved to its modern English form and has been used to refer to the auditory organ of humans and many other animals.

The ear plays a crucial role in the human sense of hearing, a vital aspect of communication and perception. Sound waves enter the ear canal and are channeled toward the eardrum, which vibrates in response. These vibrations are then transmitted to the inner ear, where they are detected by hair cells and converted into electrical signals that the brain can interpret as sound.

In addition to hearing, the ear also plays a role in the perception of balance and spatial orientation. The inner ear contains structures such as the semicircular canals and vestibule, which detect changes in head position and movement. The brain then uses this information to maintain balance and coordinate movement.

In many cultures, the ear also has symbolic and metaphorical significance. In ancient Egyptian mythology, for example, the ear was associated with the god Horus, who was believed to have the power of hearing and listening. In Hinduism, the god Ganesha is often depicted with large ears, representing his ability to hear the prayers and pleas of his devotees. The ear is often used as a metaphor for attentive listening and deep understanding in literature and poetry.

The human ear is fascinating because it enables us to perceive sound waves and interpret them as speech, music, or other sounds. It can also detect a wide range of frequencies, from low-pitched to high-pitched sounds. The ear's structure allows us to localize sounds and understand the direction from which they are coming.

The ear is a complex part of the human body with biological and cultural significance. It plays a crucial role in our communication and perception of the world around us. The ear has been the subject of study and fascination for thousands of years.

What is the connection between ear and communication and relationships?

The ear plays a vital role in communication and building relationships with others. Effective communication relies on speaking and listening; the ear is responsible for the latter. It allows us to perceive sounds, understand speech, and interpret nonverbal cues such as tone and inflection.

Listening is a crucial aspect of building and maintaining relationships. We value their thoughts, feelings, and opinions by actively listening to others. This can help establish trust, deepen connections, and foster empathy and understanding.

Listening skills can lead to better understanding, communication, and even improve relationship conflict. For example, if someone feels they are not being heard or understood, they may become frustrated or resentful. This can damage the relationship and make resolving conflicts or reaching compromises difficult.

In addition to listening, nonverbal communication plays a role, and the ear is vital. The tone of voice, inflection, and other auditory cues can convey emotion, intent, and meaning in speech. Hearing and interpreting these cues accurately is essential for effective communication and building solid relationships.

The ear is an essential component of communication and relationships. By listening actively and paying attention to auditory cues, we can build stronger connections with others and improve the quality of our interactions.

Effective communication is a fundamental aspect of building and maintaining connections with others. To communicate effectively, it's vital to both speak and listen. Speaking involves articulating our thoughts and ideas. Listening allows us to receive and understand the thoughts and ideas, and opinions of others.

The ear is responsible for receiving auditory information and plays a vital role in listening. It allows us to perceive sounds, understand speech, and interpret nonverbal cues such as tone, inflection, and volume. Understanding cues accurately is important for understanding the emotions and intent behind hearing someone's words.

Active listening is a crucial skill for effective communication and building relationships. Active listening involves paying attention to what someone is saying, asking clarifying questions, and demonstrating that you understand their perspective. It helps to build trust and strengthen relationships by showing that we value the thoughts and opinions of others.

In addition to active listening, the ear plays a role in nonverbal communication. For example, the tone of someone's voice can convey a wide range of emotions, from anger to joy to sadness. Inflection and volume can also communicate meaning and intent.

Active listening is essential for understanding the complete message conveyed by someone's words. Poor listening skills can cause misunderstandings and conflicts in relationships, while practical listening skills can lead to deeper connections and mutual understanding. By paying attention to auditory cues, we can better understand the emotions and needs of others, which can lead to more effective communication and stronger relationships.

The ear plays a critical role in communication and relationships. By actively listening and paying attention to auditory cues, we can better understand the thoughts, feelings, and intentions of others and build more robust and meaningful relationships.

Communication Considerations

The ear assumes a working physiology, but alternative methods of communication can help when one or both parties are deaf or mute. Deaf or hard of hearing people can use sign language interpretation, written notes, closed captioning, or assistive listening devices. The environment should be free of distractions, and lighting should be adequate. Text-to-speech software, writing, typing, or communication boards can be used for mute or speech-impaired people. Use precise language and be patient. Respect and empathy are crucial when communicating with deaf or mute people, and adaptability is necessary.

Hidden in Plain Sight

ARN

ARN – the last three letters of "YEARN."

The name Arn is a boy's name of Old French and Old German origin, meaning "eagle ruler."

ARN acronym or abbreviation

The term ARN can have multiple meanings depending on the context in which it is used.

Some of the most common uses of the ARN abbreviation include the following:

1. *Amazon Resource Name:* In cloud computing and web services, Amazon Resource Names (ARNs) are unique identifiers that reference and manage resources within the Amazon Web Services (AWS) environment. These resources can include anything from virtual machines to databases, and the ARN serves as a way to identify and access these resources uniquely.

2. *Acquirer Reference Number:* In finance and banking, an Acquirer Reference Number (ARN) is a unique code generated when a credit or debit card transaction is processed. It tracks and identifies transactions throughout

the payment processing system and can be used to resolve disputes or investigate fraudulent activity.

3. *Additional Reference Number*: An Additional Reference Number (ARN) is a unique identifier used in logistics and supply chain management to track and manage shipments. It is often used with other reference numbers, such as a purchase order number or a bill of lading number, to provide a complete picture of the shipment and its status.

4. *Australian Registered Number* (ARN) is used in the aviation industry to identify aircraft. This unique seven-digit identifier is assigned by the Australian Civil Aviation Safety Authority (CASA) to every aircraft registered in Australia.

5. *Alternative Reference Number* (ARN) used in the healthcare industry to identify specific medical procedures. This unique code is assigned to medical procedures and used by insurance companies to determine coverage and payment.

6. *Other Abbreviated ARNs*: There may be other abbreviated ARNs used in various industries or contexts, such as the Australian Registered Number (ARN) used in the aviation industry to identify aircraft or the Alternative Reference Number (ARN) used in the healthcare industry to identify specific medical procedures.

The acronym ARN refers to a unique identifier or code to track and manage various information or resources. The meaning of the abbreviation can vary depending on the industry. Understanding the precise definition and usage of an ARN is essential to interpret and use the associated information or resources properly.

The specific meaning of an ARN can vary depending on the context in which it is used.

Every day new acronyms show up with the same combination of letters.

Here are a few ARN acronyms I created simply for demonstration:

> ARN - All-Around Ninja
> ARN - Always Reach for Nutella
> ARN - Authenticity Reigns Now
> ARN - Always Ride or Never
> ARN - Awesome Roads Nearby
> ARN - Absolutely Radical News
> ARN - Agile Robotics Network
> ARN - Accelerated Research Nexus
> ARN - Artistic Renaissance Network
> ARN - Automated Resource Navigator
> ARN - Augmented Reality Nation
> ARN - Autonomous Reconnaissance Node

See more ARN online:
ARN - What does ARN stand for?
https://www.acronymfinder.com/ARN.html

PART V

Purpose & Mission are Led by Vision

THE phrase "find the puzzle piece" refers to the idea that some necessary skills, resources, or connections may be missing when working towards a goal.

To "find the puzzle piece" means to assess where you are currently, create a vision for where you want to be, and then figure out the steps you need to take to get there.

> *"Vision without action is merely a dream. Action without vision passes the time. Vision with action can change the world."*
>
> ~Joel A. Barker

Life offers you a multitude of paths to take. With countless options available, it's up to you to use your discernment to make the right choices that lead to a fulfilling life. Discernment means choosing an option that aligns with your values and beliefs. Identifying and filling the gaps in your personal development will help you achieve your goals and move closer to greatness, whether individual or a grand plan that is very significant.

Life is a beautiful masterpiece that you have the power to create through the art of combining different elements. It's like a giant puzzle where you place your unique patterns using your experiences, relationships, goals, and values. And just like a puzzle, there may be missing pieces; when you find them, they can help you create your enhavim, your meaningful endeavor.

Having a clear vision is essential, but it's not enough on its own.

Without taking action, a vision remains just an idea or dream that never becomes a reality. Similarly, taking action with a clear vision and purpose can save time and effort.

There is a difference between an enhavim and a goal or objective, which will be explained on the following pages. The critical difference between a goal and an enhavim is 'scale.'

Having a clear vision of your goal and taking deliberate steps towards it can help you significantly impact the world.

It is only when a clear vision paired with intentional purpose and a mission of consistent action that you have an enhavim.

Engaging in *an enhavim, a meaningful endeavor,* can lead to positive outcomes and enable us to achieve great things.

Activate Enhavim

Beyond having a goal, greatness begins with a clear and compelling enhavim, also known as a meaningful endeavor.

Having a clear purpose and direction and a vision for achieving greatness can provide guidance and motivation during both good and bad times. Pursuing an enhavim endeavor can lead to significant breakthroughs and transformations in industries or even the world. It is similar to a moonshot, as both are ambitious, risky and aim to achieve something never done before.

What is the difference between a goal and an enhavim? The best way to illustrate this is two examples, one for setting a GOAL and one for setting an ENHAVIM.

A. Setting a GOAL: Lose 20 pounds in 6 months -

Here are some steps to achieve the goal of losing 20 lbs. in 6 months:

1. *Set a goal:* Losing 1-2 lbs. weekly is healthy and achievable. Aim for a total loss of 20 lbs. in 6 months, which means losing about 3-4 lbs. per month.

2. *Develop a meal plan:* Focus on a balanced diet that includes whole foods, plenty of vegetables and fruits, lean proteins, and healthy fats. Reduce your intake of processed and high-calorie foods.

3. *Track your calorie intake:* Keep a food diary and track the daily calories in a calorie calculator to determine the

number of calories you need to finish each day to achieve your weight loss goals.

4. *Exercise regularly:* Engage in regular physical activity to burn calories and maintain a healthy weight. Aim for at least 30 minutes of moderate-intensity exercise, such as brisk walking or cycling, five days a week.

5. *Strength training:* Add strength training exercises to your routine to build muscle mass and increase metabolism.

6. *Drink plenty of water:* Stay hydrated by drinking at least eight glasses of water each day. Water can also help you feel full and reduce your appetite.

7. *Monitor your progress:* Regularly monitor your progress by weighing yourself once a week and taking body measurements. Celebrate your successes along the way to stay motivated. Weight loss requires a lifestyle change, so be consistent in your efforts to achieve your goals.

B. Setting an ENHAVIM: Win Mr. ~ Ms. Olympia

Define your enhavim to qualify for Mr. ~ Ms. Olympia, the most prestigious bodybuilding competition in the world. The passion and pursuit of an enhavim of this stature require effort, dedication, and time.

1. *Develop a solid workout routine:* This involves weight training, cardio, and other exercises that help build muscle, improve endurance, and reduce body fat.

2. *Focus on nutrition:* A proper diet is essential for building muscle and maintaining a low body fat percentage. This

involves consuming adequate protein, carbohydrates, and healthy fats while limiting processed foods, sugars, and unhealthy fats.

3. *Hire a coach:* Working with a qualified coach can help you develop a personalized training and nutrition plan tailored to your specific needs and goals.

4. *Compete in local and regional bodybuilding competitions:* Winning these competitions can earn you points towards qualifying for Mr. ~Ms. Olympia.

5. *Continuously improve:* It takes years of training, competing, and improving to qualify for Mr. ~ Ms. Olympia. You need to constantly work on building muscle, improving your physique, and mastering your posing and presentation skills.

6. *Maintain a healthy lifestyle:* Getting enough sleep, managing stress, and avoiding drugs and other harmful substances are all crucial for building a healthy and sustainable physique.

7. *Be patient:* It may take several years of consistent hard work and dedication to qualify for Mr. ~ Ms. Olympia and reach this level of competition.

To achieve your enhavim, it's difficult to say how long it would take to qualify for Mr. ~ Ms. Olympia, as it depends on factors such as your starting point, genetics, training intensity, and competition results. This process can take years of dedicated effort and focus and involve building and maintaining large muscle mass while reducing body fat to optimum levels.

The difference between a goal and an enhavim is 'scale.'

Losing weight over six months involves a gradual reduction in calorie intake and increased physical activity, leading to a slow and steady weight loss, generally between 10-20% of a person's body weight.

Training to compete as a Mr. ~ Ms. Olympia bodybuilder involves a rigorous and highly specialized weightlifting regimen, nutrition, and supplementation.

The difference in scale between goal and enhavim is significant, as is the level of effort and dedication. While losing weight over six months is a challenging but achievable goal, compared to training to compete as a Mr. Olympia bodybuilder requires commitment and discipline beyond what most individuals can realistically achieve.

Derivation of the word *ENHAVIM*

ENHAVIM is pronounced: **on-ha-veem.** Say this simple phrase, *"From Dream to Enhavim"* to remember the pronunciation.

- **EN** "near, at, in, on, within," Greek
- **HA** "breath" source of life, Hawaiian
- **AVI** "aviv" – life, French "joie de vivre," joy of living
- **VIM** "strength, energy with vigor or desire," Latin

This will be repeated in a few pages.

ENHAVIM:

Your Future Vision

Fueled by Purpose

Fulfilled by Mission

ENHAVIM combines vision + purpose + mission.

Purpose and mission led by vision.

Have you ever had a big-picture vision that seems overwhelming to achieve? It could be becoming a successful actor, starting a business, traveling the world, or opening a charitable foundation.

A vision is a significant long-term goal that you aspire to achieve. It's something that guides your actions and decisions over time. Achieving a vision can take time and effort. Such an endeavor is a worthwhile pursuit that requires sustained effort and dedication.

An Enhavim that matters is a meaningful endeavor.

CREATE YOUR ENHAVIM

Purpose and Mission Led by Vision

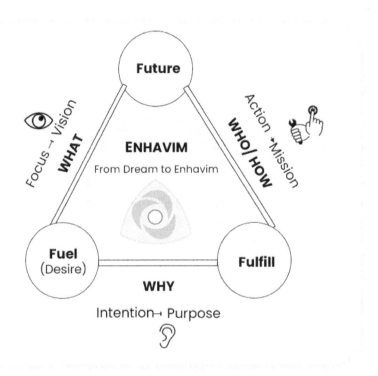

Figure 5 Enhavim: Future-Vision, Purpose-Fuel, Who-How-Fulfill

You can create a fulfilling and meaningful life by following these steps to create your ENHAVIM. The words are simple, but executing them requires dedicated time, thought, energy, and action.

1. *Define your vision:* Identify **WHAT** you want to achieve for your long-term endeavor. This vision should be aspirational, inspiring, and aligned with your values and passions. You can have more than one vision but don't get distracted.

2. *Define your purpose*: Consider what you want to achieve and **WHY** it's essential. Reflect on your unique talents, strengths, and values. Consider how you can use them to create a contribution to the world that aligns with your vision. Why do you want to pursue this endeavor; what motivates you to achieve it?

3. *Define your mission*: Based on your vision and purpose, identify specific goals or objectives that will help you fulfill your more significant purpose. These goals aligned with your vision and purpose are **HOW** you achieve it and are actionable and measurable. **WHO** else can help with this enhavim? This is where the action happens.

4. *Develop an **ACTION PLAN***: You have identified the skills, traits, habits, mindset, and people you need; next is the plan—which ties into the mission with the "how" and "who" of your endeavor. Outline the tasks, timelines, and milestones needed to achieve your enhavim. Be flexible and adaptable to changes as you progress towards your enhavim.

5. *Build a support system*: ***WHO PLAN*** - Surround yourself with people who share your values and can provide support, encouragement, and feedback on your enhavim. Seek out mentors who can provide accountability and guidance.

6. *Identify positive habits*: What positive **ACTION** habits will help you progress towards your goals over time? These habits should be consistent, aligned with your values, and focused on the long-term enhavim. Adjust and improve habits as needed.

7. *Continuously learn and grow*: Transformative **ACTION**. Stay curious and seek opportunities to learn and develop new skills related to your enhavim. This could involve getting a coach, taking courses, or attending workshops.

8. *Monitor your progress*: Regularly monitor your progress to ensure you're on track with your plans. This is a Review **ACTION**. Prioritize your tasks based on their importance and deadlines. Focus on the most critical tasks first.

By following these steps, you can set yourself up for success in creating a worthwhile enhavim. By aligning your habits with your vision, purpose, and mission, you can create a sustainable way to progress toward your enhavim while experiencing fulfillment and meaning.

Creating an enhavim is a great way to express your five core values. When your enhavim aligns with your values, it can give you a sense of purpose as you take action and progress. The YEARN advantage helps you make decisions and shape your behavior based on your values. For instance, if you want to make a positive change in the world, you can create an enhavim that aligns with the five core values. This enhavim will give you a sense of purpose and direction as you work towards achieving it. Challenges may arise, but having an enhavim will guide you towards the right path and help you adjust to stay on track.

For a compelling visual infographic of enhavim and other free resources, *visit* **www.BeLegacyWorthy.com/gifts**

ENHAVIM

(on ha veem) (n.)
a meaningful endeavor

Top three in hierarchy:
Future **vision**,
Fueled by **purpose**,
Fulfilled by **mission**.

Followed by:
strategic plan, goals, projects,
schedule, tactics, tasks, and
sequences of actions.

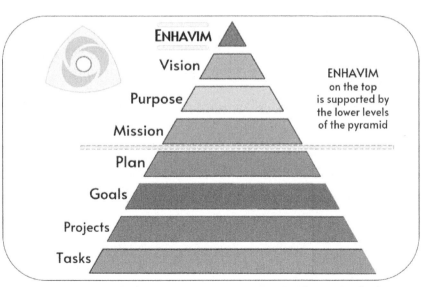

Your Future Vision · Fueled by Purpose · Fulfilled by Mission

Figure 6 Enhavim Hierarchy

> *An Enhavim that matters is a meaningful endeavor:*
>
> **Your Future Vision · Fueled by Purpose · Fulfilled by Mission**
>
> Imagination captured and idealized becomes a VISION.
>
> Vision with reason and intention becomes a PURPOSE.
>
> Purpose that benefits specific people becomes a MISSION.
>
> Mission with objectives, goals, and defined dates becomes a PLAN.
>
> Plan backed by action will manifest your *ENHAVIM*.

Derivation of the word *ENHAVIM*

ENHAVIM is pronounced: **on-ha-veem.** Say this simple phrase, *"From Dream to Enhavim"* to remember the pronunciation.

- **EN** "near, at, in, on, within," Greek
- **HA** "breath" source of life, Hawaiian
- **AVI** "aviv" – life, French "joie de vivre," joy of living
- **VIM** "strength, energy with vigor or desire," Latin

FINAL
TOUCHES

Explore Human Desire

Many authors and trainers have explored human desire and motivation.

The YEARN advantage stands on its merit; and has been elevated and lifted by the knowledge and influence of the pioneers.

The expression "shoulders of giants" acknowledges previous generations' or individuals' work and achievements. It is essential to recognize the contributions of others in the same field and value their work. It reminds us that we are all part of a larger community of thinkers and doers striving to advance our understanding and improve humanity and the world around us.

These books are found on many bookshelves and digital libraries and are worth exploring. Their lists of desires may differ depending on their focus and perspective.

1. *"Man's Search for Meaning"* by Viktor Frankl. A memoir that chronicles the author's experiences as a prisoner in Nazi concentration camps during World War II. Frankl reflects on the importance of finding meaning and purpose in life, even amid extreme suffering and adversity. The book is considered a classic of existential literature and a testament to the resilience of the human spirit.

2. *"How to Win Friends and Influence People"* by Dale Carnegie is a self-help book that provides practical advice on becoming more successful in personal and professional

relationships. Carnegie emphasizes the importance of listening, showing appreciation, using someone's name in conversation, and avoiding criticism, among other key strategies.

3. *"The Prophet"* by Kahlil Gibran is a book of poetic essays that discusses important life themes such as love, marriage, children, joy, sorrow, freedom, and beauty. The book takes the form of a conversation between a prophet, Almustafa, and the people of a city as he prepares to depart. Through his words, the prophet shares his wisdom and insights on living a fulfilling and meaningful life, urging people to embrace their individuality, seek knowledge, and connect with their inner selves and the world around them. The book is widely regarded as a classic of spiritual literature and has been translated into over 50 languages.

4. *"The Tao Te Ching"* is a classic Chinese text from the 4th century BC attributed to philosopher Lao Tzu. It is a collection of 81 short chapters or poems that provide guidance on living a meaningful and fulfilling life. Desire is a central theme; the text indicates that desire can lead to suffering and dissatisfaction. The Tao Te Ching encourages us to let go of our desires and practice detachment to find peace and contentment in the present moment. "Unattached action" is the practice of acting without effort or force in harmony with the natural flow of things. By practicing detachment from our attachments and desires and acting in connection with the Tao, we can achieve our goals with

greater ease and live a life of greater peace, contentment, and joy.

5. *"The Alchemist"* by Paulo Coelho is a novel that tells the story of a shepherd named Santiago who embarks on a journey to fulfill his legend. Along the way, he learns important life lessons about following his dreams, embracing change, and finding true happiness.

These authors and researchers have written extensively on their respective areas of expertise, and their ideas and philosophies have helped many people achieve personal growth and success.

6. Earl Nightingale - In his book *"The Strangest Secret,"* Nightingale talks about the desire for success and how it can be achieved by setting goals and taking action. Earl Nightingale's list of twelve wants resembles Napoleon Hill's list above. It includes Health, Wealth, Love, the Expression of Creative Ability, Happiness, Peace of Mind, Spiritual Enlightenment, Personal Fulfillment, Fame, Power, Authority, Social Recognition, and Immortality.

7. Abraham Maslow: Maslow's famous hierarchy of needs includes five levels of needs that people strive to fulfill: physiological needs, safety needs, love and belonging needs, esteem needs, and self-actualization needs. Maslow's self-actualization could be considered personal agency.

8. Clayton Christensen: Christensen, in his book *"How Will You Measure Your Life?"* suggests that people are motivated by three core desires: happiness, achievement, and significance.

9. Martin Seligman: The founder of positive psychology, has identified five core elements of well-being: positive emotions, engagement, relationships, meaning, and accomplishment.

10. James Allen - In his book "*As a Man Thinketh,*" he identifies seven desires: knowledge, happiness, success, passion for health, power, love, and peace. He outlines seven wishes that drive people: Health, Wealth, Love, Wisdom, Virtue, Fame, and Personal Growth.

11. Wallace D. Wattles - In his book "*The Science of Getting Rich,*" Wattles lists four primary desires: wealth, health, happiness, and love.

12. Bob Proctor - His core desires include Health, Wealth, Love, Self-Expression, Recognition, Self-Actualization, and Creative Expression.

13. Robert Collier - In his book "*The Secret of the Ages,*" Collier identifies seven desires: wealth, fame, power, love, revenge, the desire for freedom, and the desire for recognition.

14. Stephen Covey - In his book "*The 7 Habits of Highly Effective People,*" Covey outlines the desire for security, guidance, wisdom, power, and love. In "The 8th Habit" outlines four core desires: to live, to love, to learn, and to leave a legacy.

15. Brian Tracy - In his book "*Goals!: How to Get Everything You Want--Faster Than You Ever Thought Possible,*" Brian Tracy outlines the importance of setting clear goals and identifies six desires: happiness, success, love, financial

independence, health and fitness, and personal fulfillment. Tracy continues with a list of critical desires that lead to success: clarity, competence, commitment, confidence, creativity, and caring. Finally, Tracy lists six human needs: the need for certainty, uncertainty, significance, love and connection, growth, and contribution.

16. Zig Ziglar - In his book "*See You at the Top,*" Ziglar identifies the desire for peace of mind, good health, a loving family, financial security, and a sense of purpose as important desires.

17. Esther and Jerry Hicks - Esther and Jerry Hicks, in their book "*The Law of Attraction,*" list six primary desires: Well-being, Abundance, Love, Joy, Success, and Freedom.

18. Tony Robbins: Robbins has identified six core human needs that drive behavior: In his program "*The Ultimate Edge,*" Robbins identifies six core needs: certainty, variety, significance, connection, growth, and contribution. Tony Robbins' list of six human needs is similar to Brian Tracy's list, but Robbins adds the need for variety as a seventh need.

19. Vishen Lakhiani - In his book "The Code of the Extraordinary Mind," Vishen Lakhiani lists four desires that he calls "Brules" (bullshit rules) that people often hold onto Happiness, Success, Love, and Meaning. He encourages readers to question these desires and reframe them in a way that aligns with their values and purpose.

20. David McClelland: McClelland, a psychologist, identified three core motivational needs that drive behavior: achievement, affiliation, and power.

21. Edward Deci and Richard Ryan: Their self-determination theory suggests that people are motivated by three core needs: autonomy, competence, and relatedness.

22. Dan Pink: In his book *"Drive,"* Pink identifies three critical elements of intrinsic motivation: autonomy, mastery, and purpose.

23. Carol Dweck: Her work on the growth mindset suggests that people are motivated by a desire for growth and learning rather than a fixed mindset of innate ability or talent.

24. Gretchen Rubin: In her book *"The Four Tendencies,"* Rubin identifies four personality types that influence motivation and behavior: Upholder, Questioner, Obliger, and Rebel.

25. Brené Brown: Her research on vulnerability and shame identifies that humans have a deep desire for connection and belonging. She argues that vulnerability is essential to building authentic relationships with others.

In addition to the books just mentioned, you may be interested in exploring these philosophers from ancient and more modern times.

Socrates (Greek), who lived before Plato and Aristotle, is often considered the founder of Western philosophy. He is known for his method of questioning, which he used to challenge his fellow Athenians' beliefs and encourage them to think critically about the world around them. Socrates believed that the pursuit of wisdom and virtue was the highest goal of life and that this could only be achieved through self-examination and the cultivation of reason and ethical behavior. Despite being sentenced to death by the Athenian authorities for his beliefs, Socrates became a symbol of philosophical inquiry and the search for truth that continues to inspire philosophers today.

Plato (Greek) was highly abstract and idealistic, as reflected in his writings such as "The Republic" and "The Symposium." He believed that the world we see around us merely reflects a perfect, eternal realm of Forms, which can only be apprehended through reason and intellectual inquiry. For Plato, the ultimate goal of philosophy was to gain knowledge of these Forms and to use this knowledge to guide one's life and society toward more incredible goodness and justice.

Aristotle (Greek), a Plato student, had a more practical approach to philosophy. He believed that the world around us is accurate and that knowledge can be gained through observation and empirical study. Aristotle's philosophy focused on understanding the natural world and the relationships between different life forms. He also believed in the importance of logic and reason as tools for understanding the world and developing a practical, commonsensical approach to life.

Epicurus (Greek) was a philosopher who emphasized the pursuit of pleasure and happiness as the ultimate goal of life. He believed the key to happiness was to live a simple life, be free from fear and pain, and cultivate friendships with like-minded individuals.

Confucius (Chinese) was a philosopher whose teachings focused on ethics, morality, and social order. He believed in the importance of education, personal responsibility, and the cultivation of virtue in both individuals and society.

René Descartes (French) was a philosopher often called the father of modern philosophy. He is best known for his method of doubt and his famous statement, "I think, therefore I am." Descartes believed that knowledge could be attained through reason and that the human mind was separate from the physical world.

Friedrich Nietzsche (German) was a philosopher who rejected traditional morality and religious beliefs and championed individualism, creativity, and the pursuit of power. He believed that the strong should dominate the weak and that individuals should strive to become the Ubermensch or the "superman."

Thomas Aquinas (Italian) was a philosopher and theologian who sought to reconcile faith and reason. He believed that human reason could understand God and the natural world and that faith and reason were complementary. Aquinas is best known for his Summa Theologica, a comprehensive work on Christian theology.

#tyadvantage

Be Legacy Worthy

> You owe it to your future self to live your legacy by seeing your life today through the lens of "legacy-worthy" ideas, actions, and speech. Use this perspective to enhance your YEARN advantage. *#belegacyworthy*

Your Legendary Life awaits YOU! Step into your next role as you strive to 'be legacy worthy' in your thoughts, words, and deeds. Legacy is about living, creating something that will live forever *beyond you* and *because of you.*

To "be legacy worthy" is about living life to the fullest while contributing to the future. It means your life and reputation today. It's a vision that transcends one's individual lifetime and strives to create a positive impact that will last for generations.

In the business world, the role of the *Chief Legacy Officer* focuses on creating a legacy that will benefit the company in a myriad of ways. The *Chief Legacy Officer* is responsible for ensuring that the company's enhavim, or chief aim is perpetuated beyond the tenure of its current leadership.

The *Chief Legacy Officer* ensures that the company is constantly moving towards a legacy-worthy future, clearly understanding its purpose and a plan to achieve it. The role requires a deep understanding of the company's history, values, and culture and the ability to inspire and lead others toward a common goal. This fosters innovation, collaboration, and growth while staying true to the company's values and traditions.

In one's personal life, being a *Legacy Chief* means taking on the role of the leader of the family legacy. The Legacy Chief is responsible for creating a family legacy that reflects their values, culture, and traditions. This involves addressing complex topics that are often avoided or misunderstood and taking steps to ensure that the family's legacy is positive and inspiring for future generations.

The role of the *Legacy Chief* is critical in preserving and passing on family traditions and values. By proactively addressing these topics, the Legacy Chief can ensure that the family's legacy is a source of inspiration, bringing family members closer together and strengthening their bond.

Being a *Legacy Chief* or *Chief Legacy Officer* requires a commitment to making a positive impact that extends beyond oneself. It requires a vision for the future and a willingness to take action toward creating a legacy that future generations will value. You are invited to visit the Chieftain Tribe mastermind. This is an excellent opportunity to connect with like-minded individuals and learn from others who share a similar vision for creating a lasting impact.

Discover more:

www.BeLegacyWorthy.com/gifts

www.ChiefLegacyOfficer.com

www.LegacyChief.com

Famous Fives

IN addition to the Five Core Values of Y.E.A.R.N., represented by the five apple slices, many other things are organized into five sections. Items divided into five parts are called a quintile.

A quintile is one of five values dividing a range of data into five equal parts. Per the etymology dictionary, quintile dates from 1951 and is used in statistics to describe a division of data points into five parts of equivalent size.

Originating in the 1610s, introduced by Johannes Kepler, a German astronomer, mathematician, and astrologer, "aspect of planets when they are 72 degrees from each other" (a fifth of the zodiac), from La Quintus "the fifth."

On the following pages, please find some famous fun fives.

1. The Five Senses: The Five Senses: Sight, Hearing, Taste, Smell, and Touch. These senses allow humans and other animals to perceive the world around them and interact with their environment.

2. The Five Zones of the Ocean: Epipelagic (surface layer), Mesopelagic (twilight layer), Bathypelagic (midnight layer), Abyssopelagic (abyssal layer), and Hadalpelagic (trench layer).

3. The Five Great Lakes of North America: Superior, Huron, Michigan, Erie, and Ontario.

4. The Five Regions of the United States: Northeast, Southeast, Midwest, Southwest, and West.

5. The Five Regions of Africa: North Africa, West Africa, East Africa, Central Africa, and Southern Africa.

6. The Five Branches of the United States Military: Army, Navy, Air Force, Marine Corps, and Coast Guard.

7. The Five Olympic Rings represent the five continents participating in the Olympic Games: Africa, America, Asia, Australia, and Europe.

8. The Five Freedoms of the First Amendment to the U.S. Constitution: Freedom of Religion, Speech, Press, Assembly, and Petition.

9. The Five Vowels in the English alphabet: A, E, I, O, and U.

10. The Five Parts of a Plot in Literature: Exposition, Rising Action, Climax, Falling Action, and Resolution.

11. Five film elements are narrative, cinematography, sound, mise-en-scene, and editing.

12. The Five Steps of the Design Thinking Process: Empathize, Define, Ideate, Prototype, and Test.

13. The Five Phases of Project Management: Initiation, Planning, Execution, Monitoring and Controlling, and Closing.

14. The Five S's of Wine Tasting: See, Swirl, Smell, Sip, and Savor.

15. The Five W's of Journalism: Who, What, When, Where, and Why.

16. The Five R's of Environmentalism: Reduce, Reuse, Recycle, Repair, and Rethink.

17. The Five Kingdoms of Life: Monera (bacteria), Protista (single-celled organisms), Fungi (mushrooms), Plantae (plants), and Animalia (animals).

18. The Five Vertebrate Classes: Fish, Amphibians, Reptiles, Birds, and Mammals.

19. The Five most important chemical elements. Most living matter consists primarily of the 'bulk' elements: oxygen, carbon, hydrogen, nitrogen, and sulfur—the building blocks of the compounds that constitute our organs and muscles. These five elements also include the bulk of our diet; tens of grams per day are required for humans.

21. Five Elements in Japanese philosophy: Earth, Water, Fire, Wind, and Void (or Sky).

22. The Five Elements in traditional Chinese philosophy: (also known as Wu Xing) are Wood, Fire, Earth, Metal, and Water. Each element is associated with a particular season, organ, emotion, and other aspects of nature and the human experience.

23. A Fifth of Liquor: A fifth is a measurement frequently used to buy and ingest distilled spirits, including whiskey, vodka, and rum. It describes a bottle that holds around 750 milliliters or one-fifth of a gallon. *(You may need a drink after reading this list)*

24. The film *The Fifth Element* identifies four classic elements in nature: fire, water, earth, and air (referred to as "wind"), plus the power of the Fifth Element (Supreme Being) that occurs when the classic four elements are simultaneously activated and form the "Divine Light."

25. The Five Stages of Dying: denial, anger, bargaining, depression, and acceptance, defined by Dr. Elizabeth Kubler-Ross in 1969.

26. The Five Regrets of the Dying, 2019 book by Bronnie Ware. The shorter, positive versions: Be authentic, work less, express fully, cultivate relationships, and choose happiness.

27. The Five Types of Musical Instruments in Indian Classical Music: Strings (Tanpura and Veena), Wind (Flute), Percussion (Tabla and Mridangam), Brass (Trumpet), and Keyboard (Harmonium).

28. The Five Branches of Traditional Chinese Medicine: Acupuncture, Herbal Medicine, Massage (Tui Na), Exercise (Qi Gong-Tai Chi), and Dietary Therapy

29. The Five Classics of Taoism: Tao Te Ching, Chuang Tzu, Lieh Tzu, Huainanzi, and Neiye.

30. The Five Virtues of Bushido in Japanese Samurai culture: Rectitude, Courage, Benevolence, Respect, and Honesty.

31. The Five Books of Moses (Pentateuch) are central to Jewish and Christian Bibles; Genesis, Exodus, Leviticus, Numbers, and Deuteronomy.

32. The Five Pillars of Islam: The Five Pillars of Islam are the five essential acts of worship central to Islam. Shahada (Declaration of Faith), Salat (Prayer), Zakat (Charity), Sawm (Fasting), and Hajj (Pilgrimage to Mecca).

33. The Five Classics of Confucianism: Book of Changes (I Ching), Book of History (Shu Jing), Book of Poetry (Shi Jing), Book of Rites (Li Ji), and Spring and Autumn Annals (Chunqiu).

34. The Five Classics of Yoga: Hatha Yoga Pradipika, Bhagavad Gita, Yoga Sutra, Shiva Samhita, and Gheranda Samhita.

35. The Five Levels of Soul: In Kabbalah, from man's service to and in communion with God. There are five levels of awareness in ascending order: Nefesh (animalistic life force), Ruach, Neshama, Chaya, and Yechida (the essence of the soul).

Acknowledgments

The one person who deserves major kudos is **PATRICIA KROWN**.

Patricia is highly evolved and says, *"Everything about me spontaneously adjusts, corrects, and recalibrates itself to my optimum state."* Her keen eye for the manuscript has helped shape the text. She often refers to Stephen Russell's continuum.

There are no ends, no starts, just a continuum

Sure, there are doors, but it's theater, its art,

and all you do is play your part

All you do is play your part.

Many other wonderful people are recognized in the creation of this book and can be found here:

www.bookacknowledgements.com/yearnadvantage

Afterword

A S you come to the end of *'Mastering the 5 Core Values: The YEARN Advantage'*, ideally, you have new knowledge and fresh motivation that can assist you in accomplishing your objectives and fulfilling your enhavim.

YOU yearn for growth and purpose,
Thrive with courage, do so with service.

The ENVIRONMENT around you shapes your soul,
Build spaces of peace that make you whole.

ACT upon goals with determination,
Step by step, toward your destination.

RESOURCES at hand, use with care,
Tools and assets create beyond compare.

NETWORKS and community share an enhavim,
Finding strength in unity, behold a common dream.

Master YEARN's values to set you apart.
Embrace God's love, witness His universal art.

The acronym Y.E.A.R.N. represents five core values. At its core, Y.E.A.R.N. is about cultivating a strong sense of self and advocating for what matters most to you to help you express your full potential.

By embracing these core values, you can lead a more meaningful and purpose-driven life while also making strides toward achieving your greatest aspirations. Throughout this book, you were challenged to examine your core values and how they influence your thoughts, decisions, and, ultimately, your destiny.

In Part V, you were introduced to a fresh approach to goal setting, highlighting the vital role of vision, purpose, and mission in creating a satisfying and impactful journey. Embrace your boldest dreams, take risks, and go for your enhavim!

As you conclude this book, take some time to reflect on the insights you have gained and how you can apply them to your own life. Think about how you can incorporate the YEARN Advantage into your personal and professional growth and share your newfound wisdom with others. Inspire and empower those around you.

Finally, thank you for taking the time to read *'Mastering the 5 Core Values: The YEARN Advantage'*. Remember, the journey is never over; there is always more to learn and discover. Keep YEARNING for excellence and keep growing!

Yours truly,

Sherrie Rose

Free Gift

AS a token of appreciation for your enthusiasm and support, the book publisher is offering a free gift to eligible readers who have read the book. Although the specific gift is not described, it is sure to be a pleasant surprise for those who qualify. This highly prized digital download and additional resources are a way for the publisher to show their gratitude to the audience of enthusiastic book readers.

www.BeLegacyWorthy.com/gifts

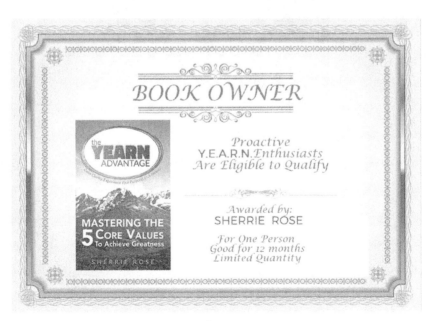

#tyadvantage

For your free copy of the visual infographic of enhavim
and other resources, go to:

www.BeLegacyWorthy.com/gifts

Author: SHERRIE ROSE

Sherrie Rose Helps Leaders Shape Tomorrow's Destiny.

She's a dynamic and forward-thinking "Chief Legacy Officer" who inspires friends and business associates to live a "legacy worthy life." Sherrie has become a sought-after authority in her field with her expertise in shaping and fulfilling masterworks led by a powerful vision.

Her inspiring journey to becoming a Chief Legacy Officer (CLO) is chronicled in her captivating book, The Cocoon Conundrum. Through her transformational experiences, Sherrie gained a new perspective and shifted her focus to become a visionary leader dedicated to creating a positive impact. As an Ambassador to CLOs, Sherrie is passionate about sharing her knowledge and expertise.

Over the years, she has engaged private webinar clients and hosted online summits as an executive producer and presenter, sharing her insights and inspiring others to reach their full potential. Her book, *The Webinar Way*, is a testament to her expertise in this field. Sherrie has also been part of the winning teams running major events such as the Olympics, Universiade, and TEDx.

Sherrie's professional qualities are admirable. She is trustworthy, committed, loyal, dependable, and a consummate professional. Her approach is confident and diplomatic, making anyone she works with look fantastic. Sherrie's natural ability to simplify and optimize systems makes her a highly sought-after professional.

One of Sherrie's standout qualities is her commitment to action. When she commits to something, it is as good as done. She focuses on scale and efficiency and does not let obstacles, delays, or excuses get in her way. Her attention to detail and focus on the big picture - the Enhavim - make her an entrepreneur who delivers results.

When working with Sherrie, individuals and businesses can count on her 100%. She is a high achiever and performer who has admirable standards. Sherrie helps guide the direction of tomorrow by encouraging others to *be legacy worthy today.*

Connect with Sherrie

- https://ChiefLegacyOfficer.com
- https://BeLegacyWorthy.com
- https://www.facebook.com/sherrieroseauthor
- https://www.facebook.com/sherrierose
- https://www.linkedin.com/in/sherrierose
- https://twitter.com/sherrierose

SHERRIE ROSE
Chief Legacy Officer
Helping Leaders Shape Tomorrow's Destiny